Bored? Lonely? Looking for intimacy? Look no further. Get this book and leave your boring, not-so-intimate marriage behind. You'll laugh, you'll fix your mistakes, and best of all...you'll start living happily ever after!

—David and Claudia Arp
Authors, The Ten Great Dates Series
and *The Second Half of Marriage*

You and your spouse can live happily ever after! Dr. David Clarke says so, and he will show you exactly how to get there. Leave behind your ho-hum, boring relationship and create a fun, passionate one.

—Pat Williams
Orlando Magic Cofounder
and Senior Vice President

Need to crack the female code or reduce selfishness in your man? In your hands you hold a question-and-answer key to turn your boring, routine marriage into a happily ever after. Based on hours of counseling husbands and wives, the authors will help you and your spouse experience intimacy once again. Get ready to laugh and learn!

—Arlene Pellicane
Author, *31 Days to a Happy Husband*

WHAT HAPPENED
TO
Happily
Ever After?

DAVID E. CLARKE, PhD
WITH WILLIAM G. CLARKE, MA

Most Charisma House Book Group products are available at special quantity discounts for bulk purchase for sales promotions, premiums, fund-raising, and educational needs. For details, write Charisma House Book Group, 600 Rinehart Road, Lake Mary, Florida 32746, or telephone (407) 333-0600.

What Happened to Happily Ever After?
by David E. Clarke, PhD, with William G. Clarke, MA
Published by Siloam
Charisma Media/Charisma House Book Group
600 Rinehart Road
Lake Mary, Florida 32746
www.charismahouse.com

Cover design by Lisa Rae McClure
Design Director: Justin Evans

Visit the author's website at www.davidclarkeseminars.com.

Library of Congress Cataloging-in-Publication Data:
Names: Clarke, David, 1959-
Title: What happened to happily ever after / by David E. Clarke, PhD, with
William G. Clarke, MA.
Description: First edition. | Lake Mary : Siloam, 2016.
Identifiers: LCCN 2015039633| ISBN 9781629986937 (trade paper) | ISBN 9781629986944 (e-book)
Subjects: LCSH: Marriage--Religious aspects--Christianity.
Classification: LCC BV835 .C57555 2016 | DDC 248.8/44--dc23
LC record available at http://lccn.loc.gov/2015039633

First edition

16 17 18 19 20 — 987654321
Printed in the United States of America

To Sandy, the most wonderful
person in the world.

By God's grace and with hard work,
we are living happily ever after!

CONTENTS

INTRODUCTION

RECENTLY I WATCHED a Disney movie with my wonderful three-year-old granddaughter, Izzy. It was a classic story of a princess and a prince falling in love, getting married, and living happily ever after.

Izzy (her real name is Isabel) has an attention span of about five minutes. She typically runs from one activity to another all day long. But she sat still, absolutely enthralled, for the entire hour-and-a-half movie!

Izzy loved the movie. She loved the sweet, beautiful princess. She loved the handsome, brave prince. Most of all, she loved the incredibly happy ending. Izzy wants to live happily ever after with her future prince, and I don't blame her.

I want a happily-ever-after marriage too! So do you. So does everyone who gets married. I believe God has put this dream in the hearts of all brides and grooms. He devoted one whole book in the Bible—the Song of Songs (also called the Song of Solomon)—to this kind of deeply intimate, forever love relationship.

It is God's desire for every couple to live happily ever after.

Unfortunately in the real world very few couples live out the happily-ever-after dream. Very few.

Just a couple of years into marriage, the dream gets seriously frayed around the edges. You realize with dismay that your marriage is not even close to the fairy tale love you had in mind. Instead of, "And they lived happily ever after," your marriage could be described by one of these tag lines:

- "And they were OK ever after."
- "And they were happy some of the time ever after."
- "And they tried to be close ever after."
- "And they hung in there ever after."

No one would put these words on a plaque and mount it in their home.

Is this the kind of marriage you want to have? Of course not. Disney wouldn't make a movie about this kind of marriage.

But I have good news. I am in the "happily ever after" business. I'm a Christian psychologist who specializes in helping couples with relationship problems. For the past twenty-five years, I've worked with couples in therapy, presented marriage seminars, and written books on marriage. I'm still a full-time therapist, working with couples five days a week. I've been married to Sandy for thirty-three years, and we have learned a lot together.

My writing partner is my dad, William G. Clarke. He has over thirty years of experience as a marriage and family therapist. Dad also spent years doing marriage seminars. He and my mom, Kathleen, have been married for sixty years.

Together we can help you take your relationship from where it is now to happily ever after. We have based this book on three pillars: the Bible, our experience working directly with couples in therapy, and what we've learned in our own marriages.

If you're OK with a boring, mediocre marriage (or worse), put this book back on the shelf or give it to a friend. If you want a terrific marriage, you have the right book in your hands. Here's the road map we'll follow.

In part 1 I explain how you built a boring marriage. You did it the same way almost all couples do. You acted out the rituals in the standard Anti-Intimacy Male-Female Contract.

In part 2 I expose the top ten intimacy-killing mistakes most couples make, and I show how to correct them. When you correct these mistakes, you'll get the deep intimacy you've been missing.

In each chapter I include a "Dialogue" section. These are conversations I've had with actual clients (no names or identifying features, of course) in my therapy office in Tampa, Florida. These dialogues reveal the main obstacles to intimacy.

At the end of each chapter (and sometimes both in the middle and at the end), you'll find a "Build Your Happily-Ever-After Marriage" section. These sections contain specific questions and action steps that will help the two of you apply my strategies.

In part 3 I'll help you dump your boring rituals, get rid of your intimacy substitutes, and create a spontaneous and exciting love.

If your spouse won't read this book—and some won't—that's OK. You'll read it, you'll change, and your marriage will change.

You'll notice a lot of humor throughout the book—at least, I think it's humor! When a book is fun to read, the principles in it are communicated more effectively. Sometimes my sense of humor is a little wacky. Off the wall. Edgy. But Izzy likes it, and I think you will too.

I need to warn you right up front that I will be hard on both wives and husbands. You each will take your turn in the hot seat. I won't pull any punches. I'll be direct and honest. That's how I do therapy, and that's how I write. That's the approach I needed—and still need. You need the truth, or you won't change. I don't mean to offend, although at times I will. I mean to get your attention, motivate you to act differently, and show you how, with God's help, you can build the marriage you want and God desires you to have.

I know you're ready to start building your happily-ever-after marriage. Turn the page and let's get to it.

PART I

How You Built a Boring Marriage

Chapter One

BOREDOM: THE NUMBER-ONE MARRIAGE KILLER

The gibbon is a small primate found in Southeast Asia. It is one of the few mammals that mate for life. When two gibbons decide to tie the knot—*boom!*—it's permanent. These miniature apes take "until death do us part" seriously.

I know what you're thinking: "Have I picked up a *National Geographic* book on apes by mistake?" In a way, you have. But this is going to be about marriage. Trust me.

Few human beings are aware of the day-to-day life of the married gibbon couple. You will now join that privileged few. I can sense your excitement. Not only will you be able to amaze your friends with your knowledge, but you'll also learn something very significant about your own marriage.

Come with me to the forests of Southeast Asia.

Just a Couple of Crazy Gibbons

After a courtship that can last months, the male and female gibbon become a couple and move in together. They leave their families of origin and settle down in an area of leafy trees, choosing one specific tree for their home tree. Once they move into their home tree, the gibbons begin to practice a daily routine they will follow without variation for the rest of their lives together.

Each morning, just before dawn, the male and female gibbons rise and sing. Together, they belt out a song that can last up to two hours. They sing this same song the same way every morning.

The male and female gibbon spend the rest of their day swinging from tree to tree in their area looking for food. When they find food, they go through a cycle of eating, grooming, and resting. They groom each other the same way every time—the left hand parts the hair, and the right hand picks through it and cleans.

Believe me, you're going to find this information helpful.

Every evening, the gibbons return to their home tree and groom each other again the same way. Sometimes they have sex.

You've always wondered how gibbons have sex, haven't you? Well, haven't we all? Here are the titillating details.

Up in the tree, the male gibbon swings past his woman several times to indicate his interest. Taking his cue without hesitation, the female assumes the position. She never complains of a headache. She never tries to get away from him. (You see, ladies, what we can learn from the animal kingdom?) The male hangs from a branch and quickly completes the act while swinging back and forth like a pendulum. (I told you this would be exciting.) Near the end of the sex act, the female cries out in her gibbon language, "Oh, honey! Yes, yes! You are the biggest gibbon stud in the forest!"

OK, I'm just kidding about those exclamations the gibbon wife makes.

In fact, there is no passion. Just the mechanical, instinctive act. The gibbons have sex in exactly the same way every time. At the end of the evening, they hold each other in the manner they always do, and then they go to sleep.

The married gibbon couple performs these same carefully programmed rituals day in and day out for years until one of them dies.

What the Gibbons Teach Us About Marriage

Why have I described for you the daily life of the gibbon couple? What can we learn from them? Am I going to recommend that you sing together in the front yard of your home for two hours every morning? No. It might be fun, but no one has the time. Besides, the neighborhood SWAT team—I mean, the community association board—would send you a nasty letter.

Am I going to recommend that you have sex like the gibbons, with the male swinging in on a branch? Yes, yes, I am. This is the secret of a happy marriage. Actually, no. You could try it, but that's not what I have in mind.

We can learn from the gibbons that, though we are human married couples, we are just like them. We perform rituals—rigid, patterned behaviors—day in and day out for years in our marriages. Many of these rituals are in place two years into a marriage. Two years!

By describing the gibbons and their daily behaviors, I have described the typical human married couple. I may have come dangerously close to describing your relationship.

The Rituals of the Typical Married Couple

Let's take a close look at the typical couple. After a few years together, the man and woman have settled into a basic, unchanging daily routine. I could set my watch by their rituals. He's getting the morning paper…now. He's finishing his breakfast and belching…now. She's asking him how he slept…now.

This couple does the same old things every morning. They repeat the same lines at the breakfast table:

Wife: Morning, honey.

Husband: Morning, honey.

Wife: It's gonna be a hot one.

Husband: Yeah, feels like it.

Wife: Looks like rain.

Husband: Sure does.

Wife: Have a nice day.

Husband: You too.

Wife: See you tonight.

Husband: OK.

As they part in the morning, they engage in the time-honored ritual of the good-bye peck. Their lips, thinned out to hard nubs, touch for the briefest of instants. No moisture. No opening of the mouths. No warmth. No lingering of any kind. No fun, either. But that's the way they kiss good-bye. They do it the same way every morning.

This gibbon—I mean, human—couple does the same old things every evening too. She's working on dinner and getting started on some household chores. He's sitting in front of the computer. She's helping the kids with their homework and getting them off to bed. He has the television on and is zipping through the channels with his remote. She's on the phone with a friend. Now she's reading a novel before bed. They practice the same basic routine every evening.

They do the same old things every weekend. Do the yard work. Wash the cars. Cart the kids to sporting events and birthday parties. Go to the mall. Go to the grocery store. Play with the kids. Visit the grandparents. Watch sports on television. Go to church.

This couple performs these rituals over and over and over. Day in and day out. Week in and week out. Month in and month out. Year in and year out. These rituals are familiar. They're comfortable. And they're boring.

Mind-numbingly tedious. No surprises. No spontaneity. No intimacy. No passion.

No chance for happily ever after.

The Same Old Communication Script

This couple communicates—or doesn't communicate—in the same way every day. They use the same lines they've used for years! They act as if they're following the script of a soap-opera episode.

The wife tries to get the husband to open up and share something personal. She wants to stir up a little conversation. She wants to find out what's going on in his heart and mind. She wants to create some closeness. And so she asks the question she has asked for years: "How was your day?"

Reading from his script, he gives her one of the five responses he always gives:

- "Fine."
- "OK."
- "All right."
- "So-so."
- "The usual."

These male human responses are designed to provide the female human with zero information and to shut down the conversation. And that's exactly what they do. This is all part of the daily communication ritual.

The ritual usually continues with the wife making more attempts to develop some dialogue with the husband. I think you'll recognize these female conversational approaches and male responses:

> **Wife:** Did anything interesting happen today?
>
> **Husband:** No. *[Or]* Not really. *[Or]* I like to leave work at work.
>
> **Wife:** What's on your mind?
>
> **Husband:** Nothing.
>
> **Wife:** *[Asks any question that probes for information.]*
>
> **Husband:** I don't know. *[Or]* I don't want to talk about it. *[Or no response—he says nothing at all. She checks him for signs of life.] [Or]* Please, honey, not now. Let's talk about that later. *[Of course, later never comes.]*

After hitting a dead end with her questions, the wife will go to the next stage of the ritual. She'll share her own personal information about her day and life experiences. She's hoping the husband will respond with interest and join her in the conversation. Of course that doesn't happen. He faithfully follows his part of the ritual: He gives no response, acts distracted and fidgety, then asks her to stop rambling and cut to the chase. Finally he tunes her out and stops listening altogether. She catches him not listening and gets angry and hurt. Any hope for intimacy has been killed again.

In another key part of the communication ritual, the wife describes a problem she's facing with a coworker, family member, child, fellow church member, or friend. She wants her husband to listen, understand her feelings, show concern for what she's going through, and try to walk in her shoes. But that's not his script in this ritual. Instead, he uses logic and tries to fix her problem. He plays devil's advocate and tries to help her see the other person's point of view. He says incredibly unhelpful things, like:

- "These things happen."
- "I have days like that—get used to it."
- "Just suck it up and go on."
- "Relax."
- "Don't let it bother you."
- "Get a grip."
- "If you don't like your job, why don't you just quit?"

The Same Old Conflict Script

When they get angry with each other, this couple automatically moves into the "here's how we deal with conflict" ritual. They act out the same behaviors and deliver the same words every single time. And every single time, they get the same results: another unresolved conflict, simmering resentments, and a relationship that is a little colder and more distant.

Check out these classic conflict rituals.

She says those four words that strike terror in his heart: "We need to talk." His throat tightens and his bowels begin to loosen. Inside, he recoils as if she had just said, "I'm going to tie you to a chair and torture you until you scream with pain." He immediately goes into his avoidance routine. He says nothing as she talks. He does not make eye contact. He refuses to engage. He will not respond. After ten or fifteen minutes of trying to talk to him, she stops and goes into the bedroom. She's angry, hurt, and completely frustrated.

Or here's another conflict ritual. After listening for several minutes to her expressing her feelings and point of view, he calmly interrupts and informs her that she has it all wrong. Totally ignoring her feelings, he "corrects" them. After all, doesn't he know better how she feels? He proceeds to tell her in a rational, unemotional manner what actually happened. She is overpowered by his articulate, logical, and persuasive presentation. She realizes she's wasting her time, so she gives in.

In another common conflict ritual, both spouses escalate tension quickly. Both shout. Both interrupt. Neither listens. Suddenly the man has had enough and walks away. The woman becomes even angrier and follows him, continuing to make her case in a loud, sarcastic way. He locks himself in the bedroom or drives off in his car.

The husband and wife throw the same old lines at each other in every conflict:

- Do we have to talk about this now?
- You're too emotional.
- Don't use that tone with me.
- I didn't say that.
- That's not what happened!
- You're just like your mother.
- Listen to me!
- Are you through yet?
- That's not worth being upset about.
- Talk to me—say something.
- Don't walk away!

The Same Old Sex Script

It's time for the typical couple to make love. Will it be a spontaneous, playful, and unpredictable experience? No, it won't be. They will make love the same way they always do. Just like a synchronized swimming team, they'll go through the same motions. From his pinch on her bottom signaling it's her lucky night to her pat on his back when it's all over, every move and every word is carefully choreographed.

Sex is about as thrilling as washing the car or cleaning the bathrooms. It doesn't make any difference if you do those chores the same way every time. But it makes a huge difference if you follow the identical sexual routine every time. Boring. Boring. Boring.

I've heard many married couples in my therapy office describe their stale, predictable sex lives. I ask them, "Why don't you videotape your sex and then watch the tape from then on? That would be about as exciting as the real thing."

Your Rituals Are Killing Your Marriage

Now, tell me. What is the difference between this typical human couple and a gibbon couple? There is no difference. They're the same! So don't laugh at the gibbons. You and your spouse *are* the gibbons. If I took two gibbons from Southeast Asia and moved them in next door to you and your mate, you couldn't tell the difference.

With one exception.

The gibbons' rituals don't kill their intimacy. They don't have any intimacy—they're animals! The gibbons can go forty or fifty years with their rituals and never get bored or lose intimacy. They're not unhappy. There aren't any gibbon marriage counselors. Observers have not recorded a single incident of a gibbon getting tired of marriage and leaving. Ape experts have studied this in the forest.

The rituals *do* kill the intimacy of us human couples. Doing the same things the same way and saying the same things the same way kills our closeness—and the process doesn't take very long. In most marriages, intimacy is on life support two to five years after the wedding.

Husbands and wives say to me, "We fell out of love," or, "Sometimes love just dies." I say, "Baloney. Love has to be killed, and your rituals killed it. You ought to go to prison for killing your marriage. It's marriage slaughter. You didn't mean to. It wasn't premeditated. But you killed it."

Slavishly following your rituals is like eating a cheeseburger with onion and mustard at every meal. Cheeseburger at breakfast. Cheeseburger at lunch. Another cheeseburger at dinner. And doing it for months and years. After a while, a cheeseburger—once exciting—is nauseating. The pleasure and passion are gone. You know exactly how it will taste. You want to eat something different, something new, but you don't know how. The cheeseburger is all you've ever known. You've never dared try something else. So you keep eating it. You won't die of starvation, but you'll wish you were dead.

And Now, Something Completely Different

The same lines. The same approaches to conversation. The same attempts at intimacy. The same defensive maneuvers to avoid closeness. The same daily behaviors. The same kisses. The same routines. The same married life every day. You're boring each other to death when you could be exciting each other (almost) to death.

Enough is enough!

You still love each other, and that's good. But if you keep on doing the same old things the same old ways, you'll lose your love. And then you'll be in real trouble.

It's time to do something new in your relationship, isn't it? It's time to break the old patterns, get rid of the old rituals, and start fresh. It's time to get your real needs met. It's time to build a marriage that really works—for both of you.

You can still live happily ever after.

Let me show you how.

Build Your Happily-Ever-After Marriage

1. Talk about the rituals in your married life. What do you do over and over in the mornings, in the evenings, and on weekends?
2. What are your communication rituals? How does the wife try to get conversation going, and how does the husband respond? What basic communication scripts do you follow?
3. How do you deal with conflict? What is your conflict ritual—meaning, what happens when the two of you are involved in a conflict? What is the sequence of events? Which classic ritual named in this chapter most closely resembles how you two handle arguments?
4. Are you doing sex the same old way every time? How would each of you say your love life is these days?
5. Agree that you're both going to stop your rituals and start fresh. Pray—right now—for God to help you build a new marriage.

Chapter Two

THE MOST POPULAR —AND DEADLY— MARRIAGE CONTRACT

All romantic relationships begin with a contract—an unwritten, unspoken, never-discussed agreement that creates roles and rituals for the partners. This contract kills intimacy. Often, intimacy starts dying just several years into a relationship.

Every married couple has a contract. And just about every couple I've ever known—friends, family, neighbors, the thousands of couples I've worked with in therapy in the past twenty-five years, and the thousands more I've talked to at my marriage seminars across the United States—have the *same* contract.

My wife, Sandy, and I had this contract. I'll bet you and your spouse had it and probably still have it. What's it called?

The Standard, Anti-Intimacy Male-Female Marriage Contract

This contract determines how we will live together. It creates specific, rigid roles for us to play. The roles lead to the rituals. It leaves no room for spontaneity and no room for creativity.

Each of us has a script to follow. Wives follow the female anti-intimacy script, and husbands follow the male anti-intimacy script. These scripts apply to every situation, every time of the day, every interaction, every conversation, every conflict, and every sexual encounter.

The female and male scripts—and the rituals that go with them—kill every single opportunity for intimacy. Most couples never achieve intimacy because these scripts create a predictable, boring relationship. Intimacy involves an element of unpredictability and spontaneity, but the rituals embedded in the scripts make us do the same old things the same old ways.

The scripts also kill intimacy by preventing emotional and spiritual connection. The rituals are mistakes—intimacy-killing mistakes—that keep the two of you at a distance and rob you of the heart-and-soul connection you each desperately need.

Are you ready for a description of the Standard, Anti-Intimacy Male-Female Marriage Contract? Good. Here we go. I think you will recognize yourself in it.

Meet the Wife

She is a sensitive, emotional, and caring soul with a big heart. She is intuitive and can identify the needs of others. She's a real caregiver and spends a lot of time and energy meeting the needs of those close to her.

She is a talker and loves to open up and share personal information in her close relationships. No detail is unimportant when she's telling a story because all the details reveal who she is inside.

She believes three myths about men and marriage.

Myth #1: Marriage will be a continuation of the wonderful excitement, romance, and intimacy of courtship.

No, it won't be. Courtship is idealistic fantasy. Marriage is harsh reality. The truth is, your husband will start avoiding intimacy very soon after the wedding. Why? Because he's a man, and that's what men do.

Myth #2: If you keep meeting your husband's needs, he will meet your needs.

No, he won't. He'll be happy and think you're happy and that everything is fine in the marriage. The truth is, if you clean the house, take care of the kids, cook, and provide sex, he'll be convinced you are the happiest wife in the world. Why? Because he's a man, and that's how men think.

Myth #3: Your wonderful husband will intuitively know what your needs are and take action to meet them.

No, also not true. The truth is, he has no idea what your needs are. He has no clue. Because he can't identify your needs, he won't do anything to meet them. Why?

Because he's a man, and he has the intuitive powers of a rock.

The wife *has* married a wonderful man. He does love her very much. But the fairy-tale marriage she deeply desires isn't easy to achieve. If she hopes to create genuine intimacy with her husband, she has to toss out these myths and change her approach.

The Female Mind-Set

In the twenty-five years I've been a therapist, I have talked with a lot of wives in my Tampa therapy office and at my marriage seminars. I know how most wives think, feel, and act in their marriages. Plus, I've been married to Sandy since 1982. I've figured out that the female mind-set denies wives the intimacy with their husbands they desire and need.

The wife not only tries too hard to get close to her husband, she also tries in the same old ineffective ways. And she often allows her husband and others to mistreat her.

But her central and most critical mistake is that she lives in an idealistic, romantic world, a place where she strongly believes her husband ought to instinctively understand and meet her needs. I have heard these statements from so many wives:

- "Without my having to say a word, my man should just know what my needs are."

- "It's true love if my man figures out my heart's desire on his own and sweeps me off my feet."
- "Everything's spoiled if I have to tell him my needs. All he has to do is pay attention. If he really cared, he'd just know."

This female mind-set, particularly in the area of communicating needs, shows itself in conversations between wives and husbands all the time. Look at this example:

> **Wife:** *[She's at home and calls the man at work.]* Honey, I feel really sick and shaky all over. I don't know if I can make it through the day.
>
> **Husband:** I'm sorry, honey. Look, just relax and take it easy. Call the doctor if you need to. I'll see you tonight.
>
> **Wife:** Thanks for nothing! I ask for some help and get the big kiss-off! You don't care about me, do you?
>
> **Husband:** I do care. I love you. What can I do for you? What do you want?
>
> **Wife:** Oh, never mind. I'll make it. *[Hangs up.]*
>
> **Husband:** *[Thinking,* What did I do wrong? *He hears the musical theme from* The Twilight Zone. *Actually, it's* The Female Zone.*]*

Here's what happened. The woman expected the man to come home and be with her. She thought she sent the message and that he deliberately ignored it.

No! He never got the message. She didn't tell him what she wanted.

Another woman would have heard, "Come home, please." But not a man. Men are not intuitive. We miss the hidden message. If you want your husband to come home, you have to tell him, "Please come home. I need you here."

Let's listen to the same married couple a few weeks later. It's Thursday evening and they are sitting on the couch in the living room:

> **WIFE:** *[She's missing the man and wants some time with him.]* Boy, this has been a busy week. We haven't had much time together. *[Hint, hint. She's dying for him to say, "You want some time with me, don't you? How about we spend some time right now talking? I'll also take you out on Friday night on a date. I've missed you too." Is that what he says? Are you kidding?]*
>
> **HUSBAND:** Yeah, it has been busy. Sure has. Some weeks are like that.
>
> **WIFE:** *[She's disappointed and a little irritated. He didn't get the message. He didn't respond the way she wanted. She tries again with a little edge to her voice.]* Have you really missed something this week—something important? *[She's talking about herself! It's so obvious to her what she means. But not to him. Like a steer being led to the slaughter, the man doesn't pick up on the difference in her voice. He doesn't realize this is his last chance to get it.]*

> **Husband:** Let me see. Yeah, honey, there were a few things I really missed. I missed the football game on television, and I missed the chance to clean the garage. That shows how busy I was.
>
> **Wife:** *[She's angry and hurt.]* Well, it's nice to know that a football game and the garage are more important to you than I am!
>
> **Husband:** *[He now knows he's in trouble, but he doesn't know why or how it happened.]* Huh? What are you so angry about? You asked me what I missed this week, and I told you.
>
> **Wife:** Exactly. I wanted to know if you missed *me*—you know, your wife—this week!
>
> **Husband:** Oh, well, sure I missed you. *[The light has dawned, but it's too little too late for this poor sucker. It's gonna be a long night as he tries to convince the woman he does love her and he did miss her.]*

The woman thinks she made it crystal clear that she wanted personal time with him. She didn't! She didn't say that. All he heard was that they've been busy and haven't had much time together. He doesn't make the leap to the real message of her wanting time with him and wanting to know if he missed her. Most men can't make that leap.

It's a special code you ladies have. Men don't know the code!

Maybe, just maybe, a very sensitive man could decipher your code and come through for you in a miraculous way. But you didn't marry a sensitive man. Frankly there aren't many very sensitive men. Sandy didn't marry one, either.

Meet the Husband

Unlike the wife, who thinks of everyone but herself, the husband thinks *only* about himself. When the man marries the woman, it's a perfect match. She thinks about him and his needs, and he thinks about him and his needs. What could be better?

The husband figures, "Hey, we agree on the most important thing...my needs." All the man asks is that his woman meet his three basic needs.

Need #1: Food

Most men live with the constant fear of not getting enough to eat. A man who eats well is a happy man. You've heard the saying "The way to a man's heart is through his stomach." Not really. It pretty much begins and ends with his stomach. When a man is full, he won't give you his heart—just a belch and his empty plate.

Need #2: Clothing

The woman's job (of course, everything is the woman's job) is to make sure the man's clothes are clean and put away in the proper place. This is in the United States Constitution. Even the Founding Fathers knew our country could not survive unless the women met the men's clothing needs. It is nothing less than a catastrophe—second only to the woman having no clear plan for dinner—if the man cannot find a particular article of clothing when he needs it.

Here's a case in point. All day long, as she has most days, the wife has done things for her husband. She prepared his breakfast, got the kids ready and off to school, worked at her own job, cleaned the home, went grocery shopping, cooked dinner, put the kids to bed, and listened to him talk about his day.

Late in the evening, the man lays out his clothes for the next day. He opens his sock drawer and freezes. *Gasp!* He cannot believe his shocked eyes. He doesn't have any clean socks!

We know what happens at this point, don't we? He goes to his wife and gently says, "Honey, you've done so much for me today. I'm embarrassed to even bring this up. I don't seem to have any socks in my drawer. How can we solve this situation?"

Is that what he does? Not even close! The very second he sees there are no socks, he yells, "I don't have any socks in my drawer!" Panic and exasperation fill his voice. This is a serious crisis situation. His life, his whole career, teeters in the balance!

Then he grouses around the place, mumbling to himself, "I don't ask for much around here—just to have few clean socks in my drawer." If he's smart, he doesn't mumble this loud enough for the woman to hear him.

What kind of selfish ingrate would have the nerve to complain about socks when the woman has done ten thousand other things for him that day? I'll tell you who:

me. I've pulled this stunt many times. I'm not proud of it. It's a man thing I have to fight.

The husband's final need will not come as a total shock to you ladies. Brace yourselves.

Need #3: Sex

Not too shocking, is it? You knew this would be on the list, didn't you?

Women, you must understand the terrible truth about your man and sex. He thinks about sex once every seven seconds. He spends the other six seconds wondering why he's not thinking about sex. When he wants sex, it becomes an obsession. It's all he can think about. Whatever you are doing and however you are feeling makes no difference to him. He thinks, "Hey, you get to have sex with me. Isn't that enough for you?" Pitiful, isn't it?

When he feels the urge for sex—and it can strike without warning at any time of the day or night—he needs it as quickly as possible. In fact, if he can't have sex within thirty minutes, something bad will happen. He'll break out in a terrible rash. He'll start shaking uncontrollably. He'll be emotionally scarred. He'll be physically damaged. He could explode because of the awesome pressure building up in his body. He could actually die! You don't want to kill this poor man, do you?

Actually, this isn't true. It takes forty-five minutes for these bad things to happen.

The real truth is that no man ever died or was permanently harmed from sex being delayed. This attitude toward sex is part of the male mentality that is embedded in most of us men.

The Male Mind-Set

These examples provide a clear picture of how the vast majority of husbands think, feel, and act in their marriages. This male mind-set robs a husband of closeness, denies him the respect and attention he craves, and deeply wounds the woman he loves.

The central, core weakness of the man is his selfishness. It's all about him. The husband lives in a self-centered, logical world in which he expects his wife to meet his needs on demand. He is a master at avoiding intimacy. He actually has a deep need for intimacy but doesn't realize it. Because of his insensitivity and ignorance of his wife's needs, he unwittingly mistreats her over and over again.

Why Do We Kill Intimacy?

Neither partner is being malicious. No one is intentionally trying to cause hurt and kill intimacy. The husband and wife are simply acting out roles that are determined by DNA and sex-role training.

These roles are born *and* made. It is genetic. God made us this way. The female and male mind-sets and the mistakes that result come naturally. They're automatic. They're unconscious. They're just what we do.

Also, and very importantly, our parents and others in our childhood provided an early and intensely influential education concerning these roles. Moms and other women teach little girls the female mind-set. Dads and other men teach little boys the male mind-set.

In about ten to fifteen percent of marriages, these roles are reversed. This is perfectly normal. The principles in the following chapters will still apply and help you if you are in this group. Just reverse the sexes.

The Road to Intimacy

Breaking out of these anti-intimacy roles is difficult, but you must do it or you'll be stuck with a mediocre marriage at best. Mediocre marriages become miserable marriages. Miserable marriages don't glorify God. They drain all the life and joy out of both partners. And they often end in divorce.

Whether you've been married two years or forty-two years, there is a way out. A way to revive your marriage. Perhaps to bring it back from the dead. To get out of the boring rut it's been in. To be joyful. To be closer than you've ever been. To be passionate. To enjoy great sex.

To live happily ever after.

Build Your Happily-Ever-After Marriage

1. Wife, when you got married, which of the three myths about men and marriage did you believe? Do you still believe any of these myths? If so, why?
2. Wife, can you relate to the female mind-set of expecting your husband to know your needs without your making them clear to him? Why do you think you use the special code?
3. Husband, can you relate to the male mind-set of being selfish? Can you admit that, most of the time, you think of yourself and your needs first? Why do you think you do this?
4. Husband, can you admit that you avoid intimacy with your wife? Why do you work so hard to avoid it?
5. Agree now, as husband and wife, that you will:

   Read the chapters that deal with your mistakes.

   Discuss together the Build Your Happily-Ever-After Marriage sections.

   Work hard to correct your mistakes.
6. Seal this commitment right now with a prayer.

Part II

Correcting the Top Ten Intimacy-Killing Mistakes

Chapter Three

MISTAKE #1: WIFE, YOU'RE SPEAKING IN CODE

Be Clear About Your Needs

I'VE TALKED TO a lot of men in my therapy office and in my seminars, and I've heard all their complaints about their wives. One of their biggest beefs is the way wives talk in code. I've heard the same message from these frustrated husbands over and over: "Doc, I love my wife, but I can't seem to please her. I try to do things for her, but I end up being wrong most of the time. I want to make her happy, but I don't know how."

When I've spoken to the wives of these men, here's what they've told me: "My husband knows exactly what my needs are, and he simply chooses not to meet them. I feel angry and hurt, and I feel he doesn't love me very much."

This is my response to these wives: "Your original assumption is incorrect. Believe me, he couldn't name your needs if his life depended on it. He's a man. I'll work with him on that. But also, he doesn't know your needs because you don't tell him your needs in a way he can understand. Your man doesn't meet many of your needs because you don't communicate them clearly. You think you do, but you don't."

Wife, you use a special language to communicate your needs to your husband. Unfortunately he has no idea how to crack this code. The answer for you is not to hope and pray he can figure it out. You won't live that long. The answer is to correct the three code mistakes and learn to express your needs clearly.

Female Code Mistake #1: Saying Nothing at All and Expecting Your Husband to Meet Your Needs

Like most wives, you assume that your husband knows exactly what your needs are and that he simply chooses not to meet them. Without giving him any clues he can decipher, you expect him to somehow figure out what you need and come through for you. You think, "If he really loved me, he'd know what I need."

I think you're living in a fantasy world and being unrealistic and unfair to your husband.

The truth is, your husband has no idea what your needs are. Most especially, he doesn't know your deepest needs that have to do with who you really are and your view of yourself. Here's a man who was born without sensitivity and intuition. A man who doesn't even know what *his* real needs are. How in the world do you expect him—on his own—to identify and meet your needs?

Don't be Terry McKay

A good example of a woman who says nothing about her needs is Deborah Kerr's character, Terry McKay, in the famous chick flick *An Affair to Remember.* Cary Grant's character, Nickie Ferrante, and Terry fall deeply and desperately in love on an ocean liner. They're perfect for each other. Soul mates. The only catch is that each is engaged to someone else. They plan to meet in six months at the top of the Empire State Building if they still feel the same way about each other.

Terry is on her way to their rendezvous. She's right across the street from the Empire State Building when she is hit by a car and seriously injured. Poor Nickie waits for hours and hours and finally has to leave because the observation deck is closing. He's forced to assume she has changed her mind and doesn't want to be his wife.

Terry's legs are crippled in the accident, and she may never walk again. When she wakes up in the hospital after surgery, she immediately gets word to Nickie to come to her. He rushes to her bedside, and she explains what happened. Nickie holds her and assures her he loves her and wants to marry her, crippled legs and all. They get married and are very happy.

Is this what happens in the movie? Of course not! It's what *should* happen. But if you have seen the movie, you know what Terry chooses to do. In classic female fashion, she says absolutely nothing to Nickie. No call.

No note. No message through a friend. Absolutely no communication.

Nickie is in agony. His life is ruined. The woman he dearly loves didn't show up for their romantic meeting, and he has no idea why. He concludes she doesn't love him. Terry decides that because she's now crippled, she doesn't want to burden Nickie. She thinks he would not want her. So she says nothing and disappears from his life.

Why does she fail to give Nickie the option of deciding for himself? The nerve! The unmitigated gall! What kind of weird thinking is this? Did the accident cause brain damage? No. Terry is making the female code mistake of saying nothing and expecting the man to meet her needs. But how can he show his love when she won't even tell him the truth about the accident? She still loves him and wants him. But she will say nothing to help the poor guy find her and pledge his love to her.

At the end of the movie, Nickie crosses paths with Terry. As they talk awkwardly in her apartment, she reclines on the couch, and, to hide them, she has a blanket over her crippled legs. Incredibly she still says nothing to Nickie! He finally figures it out on his own and tenderly tells her he doesn't care in the least that she is crippled.

He should have said, "You're not only a cripple, you're a liar!" and walked out on her. But, of course, that wouldn't be a Hollywood ending. She puts him through unimaginable torment for months because she refused to tell him the truth about the accident.

Sandy and the laundry

My wife, Sandy, has been just as guilty of the mistake of saying nothing about needs. Here's just one example. Sandy would usually start a load of laundry on a Saturday afternoon. She'd get the washer going in the garage and then come into the house to tell me she was going shopping for a while. I'd say, "Great, honey, have a good time." She'd say, "Thanks. I will. See you later."

Sandy would leave and expect me to finish that load of laundry. The only problem was I had *no idea* she had clothes in the washer. How could I know that? She never said a word about it! Unless I happened to wander into the garage and hear the washer, I'd never know.

Sandy would come home and say to me in a sarcastic tone, "Hey, thanks a lot for finishing the laundry for me." I'd ask, with a completely straight face, "What laundry?" Sandy (I'm not kidding here) would actually think I knew about the load of laundry and had selfishly ignored it. Women! The female code!

I have finally convinced Sandy that she has to tell me about the laundry before she leaves if she expects me to finish it for her. Like most husbands, I'd be happy to meet a need *as long as I know what it is*. If Sandy doesn't tell me her needs, that's her fault, not mine.

I do try to focus on Sandy and anticipate some of her needs. Now if she leaves the house on Saturday without mentioning the laundry, I'll run to the garage to check the washer. Sometimes a load is going, and I can surprise her by finishing it. But that is a rare occurrence. The old saying "Even a blind squirrel finds a few acorns" comes to mind. You can't build a great, need-meeting marriage on those few times a year when a husband stumbles onto an unspoken need and meets it.

Female Code Mistake #2: Not Saying What You Really Mean

Sometimes the woman has told the man what she wants him to do. A least, she thinks she's told him. She actually believes she sent a crystal-clear message that only an insensitive, uncaring person could miss. The man does miss it. But not because he's an uncaring brute. She happened to send the message in female code. When he fails to meet her need, she's upset. She's convinced it's his fault. He's in trouble, and he doesn't even know why.

"I want to go to the craft class."

Check out this true story I heard recently in my therapy office.

A wife gets off the phone and says to her husband, "That was my friend, Susie. I haven't talked with her for a while. She's going to a craft class this Saturday morning. I'll bet that's going to be fun. I used to do crafts all the time." She *thinks* she said, "Susie's going to the craft class, and I want to go with her. I miss her and want to renew our friendship. Even though I enjoy crafts, it's not really about crafts. It's about our relationship. She's reaching out to me, and that feels good. Is it OK with you if I go?"

She didn't say what she thinks she said! Now, another woman would have gotten her real message immediately. But she married a man. Her husband doesn't get the message because she never sent the message. At least, not in language he can understand.

Come Saturday morning, she's an emotional wreck because she's been waiting for him to discuss the craft class with her. He has no idea what's going on. He's completely forgotten about the class! An ugly scene develops as she pours out her pain to him.

She assumes he realizes she wants to go to the craft class so she can spend time with her friend. She assumes he will offer to stay with the kids so she can go. She goes into a twenty-minute monologue about how little time she has for friends. One time—one lousy time—she has a chance to be with a friend, and he denies her the opportunity. But her assumption that he got the message in the first place is incorrect. She's built up all these painful feelings out of thin air.

Is this fair? No. Is it the way most wives operate? You'd better believe it. The woman incorrectly assumes she sends a clear message to her man. Then when he does nothing, she builds up a whole scenario in her mind about what a crumb he is. "He's this, and he's that. He feels this way or that way about me. He has the nerve to...He's such a..."

This wife was shocked out of her head when I told her she was the one who blew it in this situation. She was sure I'd confront her husband for not acting on her clear message. She was wrong. I informed her that she was guilty of using the female code and that no man on earth would have understood her "message."

Female Code Mistake #3: Getting Upset With Your Man and Refusing to Tell Him Why

Here is a marital scene repeated millions of times a day in homes across the globe.

The woman and the man are together at home, and the woman is in a funk. She's quiet, withdrawn—just not herself. After a while, the man notices that she's upset.

> **Husband:** What's wrong, honey?
>
> **Wife:** You know what's wrong.
>
> **Husband:** No, I don't know what's wrong. That's why I asked.
>
> **Wife:** Oh, you know all right. Don't play dumb with me. I know you know.
>
> **Husband:** *[He searches his small brain. He wonders,* What could it be? What have I done this time? *He comes up empty.]* I really don't know. I have no idea.
>
> **Wife:** *[She feels insulted and angry.]* Well, if you don't know, I'm certainly not going to tell you.
>
> **Husband:** *[He is bewildered and flabbergasted.]* Honey, wait a minute. Be reasonable. I don't know, so you need to tell me. Then we'll both know and we can have a normal conversation. Who knows, maybe I can help you feel better.

Sound familiar? The man can't win. Even when the woman eventually tells him what's bothering her, she's unhappy because he should have known in the first place. And by the time she tells him, she's worked up quite an emotional lather of anger and hurt.

Wife, can you see what's happening here? You don't clearly tell your man what you need in the first place. Naturally he doesn't come through, so you're upset. You don't tell him why you're upset because he ought to know. But he doesn't know what has happened! He doesn't know what your original need was, and he doesn't know why you're so offended now.

Whose fault is this? It's your fault, ma'am. Your unbreakable code has created confusion and pain. Without realizing it, you're making yourself and your husband miserable.

Maybe you can relate to some of the "justifications" that follow. This is a dialogue I have had with many female clients.

The Dialogue

Wife: We live in the same home. How can he not see my needs? They're obvious!

Me: No, your needs are not obvious. They would be to a woman. But you didn't marry a woman; you married a man. He's dense. And he's not a special case. Ninety-nine percent of men are like this. I'm a clinical psychologist, and I'm the same way.

Wife: He should know me and love me enough to figure out my needs.

Me: That's magical thinking. Stop it. He does know you, and he does love you. But that doesn't mean he can figure out your needs on his own.

Wife: Telling him spoils everything. If I state a need clearly, I'm not sure he really wants to do it. Is he doing it because he has to, or is it really the desire of his heart?

Me: Not telling him spoils everything. Go ahead and tell him, or he won't know. His response and attitude after you share the need will tell you if he's sincere.

Wife: I don't want to seem too demanding. I don't want to burden him with my needs.

Me: According to my Bible, meeting your needs is his job. But if you don't tell him what they are, he can't meet them. Then you'll resent him and be angry and pull back emotionally and physically. That behavior will put an unfair burden on him. So, assertively and nicely, tell him exactly what you need.

State Your Needs Clearly to Your Man

Your man requires the conversational equivalent of a brick to the side of the head. Saying nothing won't work. Sending a coded message won't work. Getting upset and thinking he ought to know why won't work. The only thing that will work is to tell him clearly, directly, and exactly what you need and exactly when you want the behavior accomplished.

Make sure you have his attention. A man cannot do two things at once. Don't be vague. Don't hint. Don't be coy. Don't be subtle. Use plain English. Be brief. Be specific. Like this:

> **Terry McKay:** Look, a car hit me on the way to our meeting. My legs are crippled. I still love you and want you, but I'm not sure how you'll feel about me with my physical limitations. Come to the hospital, and let's talk about our relationship.
>
> **Sandy:** I've started a load of laundry. Please finish it, fold the clothes, and put them away.

Sit down with your husband, and let him know you're sorry for not clearly expressing your needs to him and that from now on, you'll be working hard to communicate in a clear, direct way what you need from him. Tell him you'll be sharing your needs both verbally and, at times, in writing. Tell him that when you're expressing your needs in person, he has a choice: Would he rather record your needs himself on a pad he keeps for this purpose—which I highly recommend—or have you hand him the list of your needs you've written on a three-by-five card?

In this meeting about needs, you'll be explaining the four strategies I explain below.

This is your good-faith effort to get your man on board with the new need-meeting program. Ask him for input, suggestions, and ideas he may have about how to meet your needs. Since his mental abilities with regard to your needs are limited, suggest he jot on his pad the ways you tell him he can meet really important needs. Reviewing the list produces permanent learning of your needs and how you want them filled.

WIFE, HERE ARE YOUR FOUR STRATEGIES

I'm recommending you implement four concrete strategies to teach your husband your needs and communicate them in a way he can understand. Remember, he needs it spelled out for him—so you're going to do just that.

Strategy #1: Start the day right.

In the morning before you go your separate ways, tell him verbally what you need him to do for you that day. He can note your needs on his pad, or you can hand him a three-by-five card with your needs listed on it. Tell him you would be thrilled if he did these things for you by the end of the day.

For example, your list of needs might include:

- Please call the plumber and have him come between 3:00 p.m. and 5:00 p.m. today.
- Please pick up Johnny at 5:30 p.m.
- Please get eggs, marked "large," a gallon of whole milk, and angel hair pasta.
- Please call your mother and tell her we can't make it on Sunday.

If your needs change during the day, call, text, or e-mail him to let him know. For example, say:

- I can't be home for the plumber. Please reschedule it for tomorrow at the same time.
- Please add 8 oz. sour cream and tortilla chips to your grocery list.

When you see him in the early evening, tell him any additional needs you have for that night. It could sound like this:

- Please cook the pasta while I handle the rest of the meal.
- Please give Johnny a bath tonight. He should be in bed by 8:30 p.m..
- Honey, I need a ten-minute back rub.

When you're sharing these needs in the early evening, you'll probably just do it verbally. However, if he forgets too often, use the writing approach. He can jot them down on a pad or record them in his electronic device, or you may give him the three-by-five card.

I know what you're thinking: "I'm going to feel pretty dumb handing my husband a three-by-five card with my needs on it." All I can say is that you'll feel a lot worse if your needs don't get met. Your husband has no memory, so a written list is often essential. I realize lovers in movies don't use these need lists, but that's not real life!

Strategy #2: Debrief and prepare.

In your twenty-to-thirty-minute daily couple time (more on this in a later chapter), talk to him, with gentleness and respect, about how he handled your needs that day. Thank him for coming through, tell him how much it meant to you, and briefly express your feelings if he didn't meet certain needs.

If you know of specific needs you'll have for the next day, tell him. Men don't like surprises, so you will give him a heads-up. Again, he can record them for himself or take your three-by-five card. In the morning, if necessary, you may add to or subtract from the list of needs.

Strategy #3: Post your needs for the week.

Sit down on Saturday or Sunday and make a list of your needs for the upcoming week. Use seven columns for the seven days. Under each day list the needs you want met that day. Post this list of needs on the refrigerator so your husband can't miss it. You can make changes on this list as the week progresses. You'll still share your needs verbally and use the three-by-five card, but this is another effective way to communicate with your man.

Strategy #4: Confront failure.

Obviously, your husband won't meet every need you express. But these communication strategies will significantly increase the percentage of needs he does meet. When he fails to meet an important need and you're angry and hurt, you must go to him and briefly express your feelings using one-way communication.

By one-way, I mean you will do all the talking and you will ask him to listen and not respond at that time. Here's an example:

> Honey, I have something to say, and I just want you to listen and hear me out. Don't say anything. I'm angry and disappointed because you did not call the plumber and you did not get the groceries today. I was clear with those needs. The leak in the bathroom really bothers me. And I needed the sour cream for dinner tonight. I have to be honest so I can keep from getting resentful.

Say your piece, and then walk away. This process cleans your system and prevents bitterness and resentment from building up. Besides, your man may respond to your honest expression and work harder to meet your needs. If he still has time, he may take action to meet the needs you just talked about.

Practice these strategies and you will like the results. When your man knows your needs, he can meet them. You'll be happy and he'll be happy, because you're happy.

Build Your Happily-Ever-After Marriage

1. Do the three female code mistakes described in this chapter sound familiar? Tell your husband one recent example of how you did not make your needs clear to him.
2. Ask your husband to give you a recent example of how you did not make your needs clear to him.
3. What reasons or excuses do you use to avoid making your needs clear to your husband? What prevents you from being upfront and direct with your needs?
4. How did your mom share her needs with your dad? What did she teach you about sharing needs with a man?
5. Discuss with your husband the four need-meeting strategies outlined in this chapter. What do you think will happen if the two of you try them?
6. Right now, give your husband a list of needs for tomorrow (verbally and in writing). Agree to meet tomorrow evening to talk about how the need-meeting practice went.

Chapter Four

MISTAKE #2: HUSBAND, YOU'RE BEING SELFISH

Focus on Her Needs

It's dark in the home. It ought to be—it's 1:00 a.m. The married couple is in bed, both sleeping soundly. Suddenly, the man stirs and shakes the woman awake.

> **Wife:** What...what is it?
>
> **Husband:** I...uh...want to...you know.
>
> **Wife:** What are you talking about?

Oh, she knows what he's talking about. She's just stalling for time, trying to get him off track. She harbors a very faint hope that maybe he'll realize the tacky, inappropriate, and absurd situation he's putting her in.

Husband: You know, you and me. I feel like... being together. You know, making love.

Wife: *[She lights up immediately, gives him her biggest smile, and turns to face him.]* Sure, big fella. What took you so long to ask? Why sleep when I can love my man? You've made my day—and my night! Let's go!

Is this how she reacts? I don't think so. She's disgusted. Not surprised, but disgusted. Her response is usually more along these lines:

Wife: What? Oh, come on! You can't be serious. What time is it? Are you crazy? Can't you control your hormones and wait?

Whether this couple has sex or not, the wife feels used. She's not prepared in any way to be a cooperative, interested participant. She feels like nothing more than a filling station!

Sound familiar, ladies? I'll bet it does. If it's any consolation, your man isn't the only husband groping in the middle of the night. Many wives have experienced the sexual thrill of the late-night, early-morning Casanova.

Of course, as a highly trained Christian psychologist who conducts marriage seminars around the country, I would never engage in such crude, selfish behavior. When I'm ready for sex, I notify Sandy three days in advance with a romantic card on her pillow. On the day of sex, I clean the entire home from top to bottom, help the kids with their homework, cook the evening meal, and then make sure the kids are confined to their rooms. I lead my queen into the boudoir, where she is greeted by soft music and rose petals scattered on the bed.

All right, that's enough. I'm making myself sick. The truth is, I don't always do a great job asking Sandy for sex. I have improved in preparing her for making love, but I have to admit I have been guilty of midnight and early-morning touching.

Sex is just one area where I—and the rest of the men reading this—have exhibited classic male selfishness. The husband is usually not selfish in a mean-spirited, pathological way. He's not consciously and with evil intent trying to hurt his wife. His tendency to think of himself and his needs first is a genetic, automatic mechanism built into his male brain. Unfortunately he does hurt his precious wife—over and over again—with his selfishness.

Men, it's time to stop this selfishness. And I will begin my attack on the problem with some examples of selfishness from my own life.

The Miracle of the Grapefruit

I'm like many men. My mother unintentionally fostered my selfishness by spoiling me. From my birth through my high-school years, she did my laundry. She cooked my meals and supplied me with my favorite snacks. She carted me to all my sports and other activities. She nursed me when I was sick.

So my selfishness is my mom's fault.

No, not really. But her caring behavior did play a part in programming my already selfish male brain to think of myself first and expect a woman to meet my needs.

Here's an example of Mom's influence. Early in our marriage, Sandy and I were enjoying grapefruit for breakfast one morning. We were each eating half a grapefruit, using spoons to scoop out the little sections.

I said, "Sandy, isn't it neat how the grapefruit has these little spoon-sized sections you can just scoop out? It's so convenient and easy. I guess it's just one of God's little miracles."

Sandy looked at me strangely and said, "What are you talking about?"

I replied, quite innocently, "You know, the grapefruit has these small, ready-to-eat sections."

Sandy laughed out loud, nearly choking on a grapefruit wedge. "Dave, the grapefruit doesn't come off the tree sectioned. Someone has to use a knife and section it by hand. I sectioned your half twenty minutes ago, before you came to the table."

Boy, did I feel dumb. You see, my mom always had sectioned my grapefruit for me. I took that for granted, never seeing the work that caused it to happen. My meals appeared on the table. My laundry appeared in my bureau drawers. My chauffeur took me where I wanted to go. I took it all for granted. I got used to having all these jobs done for me. Why, I deserved this kind of service, and my mom seemed happy to do it.

Always Leave a Little Behind

Here's a clever and incredibly selfish strategy I have followed for years: Never completely empty any container of food so you won't have to throw it out, clean the container, replace the food item, or be accused of eating food someone else wanted.

I never finish a box of cereal. I leave a handful of crumbs and shavings so someone else is forced to finish it, throw out the box, and put cereal on the grocery list. Brilliant, isn't it? I walk away free and clear. I follow the same strategy for milk, chips, cookies, any food in a bag, and leftovers. Believe me, leaving three green beans on a plate in the refrigerator takes guts. I've even been known to leave one or two squares of toilet paper on the roll so I don't have to replace it. Sick, isn't it?

I'm Sick! Help Me!

Speaking of being sick, that's when I'm really at my selfish best. For me, being struck by an illness, even if it's just the sniffles, is a major event. I act as though I've contracted smallpox and am barely hanging on to life. I want the whole world to stop for me. I want sympathy. I want attention. I want to be served. I don't want anyone to expect me to do any chores during my recovery. I want Sandy to kindly and lovingly nurse me back to health. Is that so wrong?

Yes, it is wrong. And selfish.

Birth-Control Nightmare

Another shocking example of my selfishness occurred when Sandy was pregnant with our fourth child, William. It was a bit of a surprise. OK, it was a shock. But we recovered nicely and even began discussing the pros and cons of having a fifth child. After about ten seconds, we decided that four would be enough. But something had to be done, and quickly, or we'd end up with seventeen kids. All I had to do was look at Sandy and she became pregnant.

I naturally assumed Sandy would get her tubes tied after delivering William. I mean, wouldn't that be the easiest solution? Most of our friends had done that and seemed perfectly happy about it. Besides, how could a man who falls apart when he gets a cold possibly survive an operation where a very sharp object is used to cut his private parts? And this happens while he is fully conscious. It's barbaric! It's wrong! It's not fair! It's terribly painful! It's too expensive! (I wonder how many men have died from vasectomies.)

I was thinking all this, but fortunately I didn't say any of it to Sandy. I'll never forget the brief conversation we had when we decided on a permanent birth-control solution:

> **Sandy:** You're thinking I'm going to have my tubes tied, aren't you?
>
> **Me:** *[Being a moderately intelligent man, I said nothing.]*

Sandy: I've been through three pregnancies. I carried each child for nine months and endured the extreme pain of three deliveries—pain you would never even remotely understand. I dealt with all the aches and pains and changes in my body. And now I'm pregnant for the fourth time and will do it all over again. I ask you, Dave, what do you think we should do to prevent all this from happening a fifth time?

Me: *[In times of crisis and confusion and when Sandy has that certain look on her face, I've always found it helpful to go with this question.]* What do you think, dear?

Sandy: You'll get a vasectomy two weeks from today. Here's your appointment card. Good luck!

Me: Yes, ma'am. That was just the solution I was considering. Thank you for setting it up so quickly.

Even though I knew the vasectomy procedure was a piece of cake and nothing like vaginal delivery pain, I still had to milk it for all it was worth. I mean, I did go under the knife for my woman. I suffered pain for her. I was her birth-control hero. Actually Sandy did appreciate my effort and allowed me to get a little mileage out of my two-day recuperation. (It hurt for only a few hours, but she didn't need to know that.)

A Man's Just Gotta Have Fun!

Looking back over the years of my marriage, I've been undeniably selfish in the area of entertainment. I have controlled the television remote. I have watched too many hours of sports on television. I have chosen to play golf and go to sporting events with the guys when that time would have been better spent with Sandy and the kids.

Men like to have fun, and they tend to spend too much time indulging themselves in their hobbies: surfing the net, playing video games, watching sports on television, playing softball, shooting hoops, golfing, bowling, hunting, fishing, skiing, working out at the gym, reading the newspaper...

You'd think there would be no defense of selfishness. Oh, there is. In the dialogue box you'll find some common male justifications for selfish behavior, followed by my usual responses to them.

The Dialogue

Husband: I work hard for a living.

Me: Who doesn't? Your wife is working just as hard as you are, and she needs your help. Besides, the Bible says your most important job is meeting the needs of your wife.

Husband: I'm doing my share around the home. I carry my weight around here.

Me: What you think doesn't really matter. What matters is what your dear wife thinks. She's the one you need to please. When she says you're doing your share, you're doing your share.

Husband: I do more than my dad did and more than a lot of guys I know.

Me: Your wife isn't married to your dad or these other guys, is she? Comparing yourself to other husbands is just a way to avoid facing the reality that you're not meeting your wife's needs.

Husband: I don't hang out in bars, drink like a fish, use drugs, or chase women.

Me: Yeah, well, I hope not. I'll bet you're not a serial killer, either. You want credit for that? Your wife has higher expectations of you.

Husband: I can never please her. Nothing is ever good enough for her.

Me: Well, we won't know until you try, will we? You're probably doing things *you* think she needs. And you are probably wrong. Put together two months of solid effort meeting her actual, verbalized needs, and then we'll see if she's pleased.

Husband: She's not thankful for what she has. Lots of women would love to have the life she has.

Me: I'm not sure there would be a line out the door. I know living with you is a tremendous privilege, but that isn't the point. The point is, are you meeting her needs on a regular basis?

Why So Selfish?

There are five central reasons for the selfish streak in men. One, it's a guy thing. We're born this way. Two, our dads probably modeled selfish behavior. Three, our moms probably modeled acceptance and enablement of our dad's selfishness. Four, our moms catered too much to our needs and spoiled us. Five, our wives feed our selfishness by being too caring and nurturing.

Whatever the reasons, now is the time for change. When we focus too much on *our* needs, we fail to notice and meet our wives' needs. And that's wrong. Our selfishness hurts our wives and causes us to violate God's Ephesians 5:25 command: "Husbands, love your wives, just as Christ also loved the church and gave Himself for her." Christ sacrificed everything, including His life, for the church. Husbands, we are to sacrifice everything, including our selfish interests, for our wives. Their needs are more important than our needs.

Being selfish for the first part of your marriage is not a crime. Staying selfish *is* a crime. I have worked hard, and am still working hard, to change my selfish behavior and meet Sandy's needs. Now it's your turn.

Assume Nothing

The husband will often assume his wife is happy and satisfied if no obvious problems or disturbances are interrupting his comfortable lifestyle. He thinks to himself, *Hey, if she's cooking meals, doing the chores, taking care of the kids, and having sex with me, things must be OK.*

The husband, in his selfish way, will make this assumption: *If I'm happy, she's happy.*

Not necessarily.

The light may begin to dawn if the woman holds a gun to his head and says, "It's all over, Slimeball. I'm taking you out." At this point, the man will realize a problem exists: *Oh, I think she's a little unhappy with our relationship.*

Husband, do not assume your woman is happy and feeling loved. She could be dying inside. The fact that she continues to do the chores, cook, and have sex does not mean you are meeting her needs.

The typical husband truly believes he knows what his wife's needs are, and he's confident he's doing a terrific job meeting them. He's shocked to find out in my therapy office that he has no clue what her needs are and that he's not even close to meeting them.

I say the same thing to all the husbands I see in therapy: "Your wife defines whether or not you meet her needs, not you. If she says you're not meeting her needs, you're not meeting her needs. The only way to know her needs is to ask her...frequently."

Ask Her What Her Needs Are

Stop assuming you know her needs, and ask her. Not asking is like throwing darts in a pitch-dark room. You have no idea where the dartboard is! You must ask her often because she'll change her mind. She is an emotional, moody, and unpredictable creature.

Ask her in the morning, before you go your separate ways. Say, "Honey, what are your needs today? What can I do for you today?" We hope she'll be telling you what her needs are, but you ask anyway. When you ask, have a writing pad handy and jot down her needs. You use lists for your job, don't you? This is your most important job, so keeping a list shouldn't require a second thought.

You may choose to not write down her needs. Then you are sure to forget. She'll be upset that you forgot. She'll be upset that you didn't meet her needs. You'll be upset because she's upset. You'll have to spend the evening listening to her vent, saying you're sorry forty-five times, and trying to reassure her that you do love her. Or you may write down her needs and spend a pleasant evening with a warm, loving woman whose needs have been met by her loving husband.

By phone, ask her at lunchtime or in the early afternoon, "Sweetheart, have your needs changed since this morning? Can I do anything else for you today?" Again, write down any changes or additions on your pad. She'll love the fact that you called because it reveals that you're thinking about her. And you'll catch any new needs she may have.

Ask her in the evening as soon as you see her, "Sweetheart, I love you. What can I do for you tonight?" Jot down her needs and spend the first part of the evening taking care of them. With any luck, one of the requests may be, "Make wild love to me after the kids are in bed." If you're asking for and meeting her needs on a daily basis, this kind of request will not be out of the question.

Ask her just before bed, "Honey, do you know what your needs will be tomorrow?" On your pad, jot down what she says. That's a nice, loving way to end the day.

Husband, I know what you're thinking: "You're kidding, right? No husband I know asks for his wife's needs four times a day and writes them on a pad." No, I'm not kidding. True, very few husbands do what I am suggesting. Those who don't are the ones with unhappy, resentful, and cold wives. Those who do are following the example of Jesus: "The Son of Man did not come to be served, but to serve" (Matt. 20:28).

If You Can't Meet a Need, Tell Her Why

Your wife suffers when she thinks you ignore her and don't explain why you don't meet her needs. It's a double whammy. Her needs go unmet—that's one whammy. She has no explanation for why they went unmet—that's the other whammy.

The woman wants to know why. Not knowing bothers her. If it bothers her, sooner or later it will bother you. She may not mean to make you pay for your lack of information, but you will pay.

Sir, when your woman asks you to meet a need or when you ask her what she needs, train yourself to respond as soon as possible in one of two ways.

Response #1: Say yes with a plan and a timetable.

Write down, immediately, her need and your plan for meeting it. Make sure your wife agrees with your plan. This procedure provides your wife with peace of mind and security. It also ensures you won't blow it and fail to come through.

You might say this:

- "I'll call the plumber before noon today and schedule him to come to the house tomorrow between three and four."

- "I'll mow and edge the lawn by Saturday at six."
- "I'll vacuum the living room by the end of the evening."

Remember, when you say you'll do something for your woman, you've made a promise. If you don't do it the way you said you'd do it or when you said you'd do it, she'll feel betrayed. Trust is damaged. She'll feel unloved and unimportant. You'll have to spend time doing damage control.

Response #2: Say no with an explanation.

Your wife needs to know why the answer is no. Don't leave her hanging. Tell her right up front your reason for not meeting one of her needs. If you say yes but later realize you won't be able to meet a need, tell her as soon as possible the reason you can't do it. For example, say:

- "I'm tired."
- "I don't have the time today."
- "I'm angry at you."
- "I have something else I have to do [and tell her what it is]."
- "I didn't realize the store closed at five."

You may well have a legitimate reason to say no. You are far better off saying no with an explanation than saying yes and not coming through. No with an explanation gives her closure, and she can drop it. A woman without closure is not a pretty sight! She'll keep picking at you or stay hurt inside about it.

Get Regular Feedback

Ask your wife on a regular basis how effectively you're meeting her needs. You have to get feedback to do a good job. So when you're learning this new system, ask her every day how you're doing: "Am I meeting your needs, honey? How can I improve?"

Even after you've gotten the hang of it, ask her for feedback every few days. At a minimum, ask her once a week for an evaluation. This keeps you on track and is a great way to express love for her. Then act on her feedback.

As men, we all tend to be selfish. Without realizing it, we hurt our wives by meeting our own needs and largely ignoring their needs. It's time for change. As we identify and meet the needs of our wives, our marriages will get a lot better.

Build Your Happily-Ever-After Marriage

1. Husband, can you admit that you tend to be selfish? Tell your wife some recent examples of your selfishness.
2. Ask your wife to share a recent example of your selfish behavior.
3. What are your reasons or excuses for acting in selfish ways? Which excuses from the Dialogue section have you used?
4. Where does your selfish behavior come from? Did you learn it growing up in your home? What kind of selfish behavior did your dad model for you? Did your mom cater to you? Has your wife enabled your selfish behavior?
5. How do you think you're doing meeting your wife's needs? After you give your assessment, ask your wife how she thinks or feels you're doing.
6. Are you willing to follow the strategy I describe at the end of the chapter for asking what her needs are? Right now, ask your wife for a list of needs for tomorrow, and jot them down on your pad. Be sure to tell her your plan and timetable for meeting her needs. Agree to meet tomorrow evening to talk about how effectively you met them.

Chapter Five

MISTAKE #3: WIFE, YOU'RE TRYING TOO HARD

Talk Less, Talk Smart, and Let Him Pursue

THE COMMUNICATION PROBLEMS between husbands and wives go all the way back to birth. Our God-ordained differences are wonderful, but they get in the way of connecting on a deep level in conversation.

Most men are natural doers, not talkers, and they have a built-in drive to avoid emotional intimacy. Most women are born talkers and have a built-in craving for emotional intimacy.

A Disaster Waiting to Happen

Boys and girls grow up, but their basic differences in communication styles don't change.

The man is action oriented and conversationally challenged. He will talk, but only on a superficial level. He naturally tends to avoid emotional connection. He wants to *do* things with you: like watch the ball game or do a physical activity or share a hobby or have sex—a lot of sex. He is satisfied with a fairly shallow level of emotional intimacy.

The woman is talk oriented and conversationally focused. She wants to talk on a deeper level rather than on just an intellectual or informational level. She has an intense desire to emotionally connect. She doesn't mind doing things with you as long as you'll talk with her and create an emotional bond. She is very disappointed and hurt by the lack of emotional intimacy in your marriage. She can't be truly happy in your marriage without it.

Great combination, huh? Actually it's a disaster waiting to happen. And it does happen. Driven by these differences, the man and the woman each make critical mistakes in the area of communication and intimacy.

Because of the central importance of communication in marriage, I will address the wife's mistakes in communication and give her the tools to talk to and connect with her husband. But I don't place all the blame on her. I will also address the husband's mistakes in communication and help him talk to and connect with his wife.

Wife, brace yourself. You're going first.

Women Are Born Talkers

Sandy and I have a son and three beautiful daughters. The girls love to talk. They live to talk. There aren't enough hours in the day to handle all their words. Leeann and Nancy even talk in their sleep.

My girls talk with us and with each other. They talk on their cell phones with their friends. They talk on the computer in long, expressive e-mails. They text continually. I haven't spoken on our home phone or used my computer at home for two years. I can't get on either one. The girls' supply of conversational information is endless. My Emily will spend three hours with some friends at a party, talking all the time. When she gets home, she'll immediately start texting so she can talk with these same girls about what they just talked about.

My girls jump from topic to topic, and every topic—no matter how trivial—is important because it can lead to a whole chain of interesting conversational tidbits. Here's a recent conversation (actually, a monologue) I had with my daughter Leeann:

> Dad, that's a nice shirt you are wearing. Is that a light green stripe? My friend Bobbi was wearing a skirt two weeks ago with a light green stripe. She got into trouble with her mom because her skirt was too short. They had a bad argument out by their pool. The pool was dirty, so her mom blamed her for that too. Her little dog, Fluffy, a white and brown wiener dog who has kidney problems, came running up just then and tried to

> jump into her arms. Bobbi didn't see her coming, so she jerked back in surprise, and Fluffy jumped right into the pool. It was hilarious! You know, I saw another dog last Thursday that looked like Fluffy. By the way, did I mention that I saw Fluffy once? Bobbi brought her to school one morning. That was the same morning that I broke my favorite yellow hairbrush. I loved that hairbrush. Anyway, this other dog was wearing a cute little red and black checkered vest. My friend Ashley had bought that same kind of vest last March when we were shopping at the mall. Can you believe that? I remember the salesperson had bright purple hair, a nose ring, and a bad attitude. She was rude to Ashley and me. Oh, there were so many weird things that happened that day at the mall! We were just getting dropped off at the entrance by her mom when...

This was the first two and half minutes of the conversation! Leeann was just getting warmed up. I don't have room to list the topics Leeann covered in the other twenty minutes. You see how important noticing the green stripe was? Women talk the way paleontologists create prehistoric animal models for museums. From one chipped tooth, these scientists build an entire dinosaur. Woman can easily build an entire conversation from one tiny, inconsequential fact. Amazing!

Raised to Create Closeness

You typical woman isn't just born to create closeness. She's also raised to create it. Her mom, her grandmothers, her aunts, her sisters, her schoolteachers, and the other significant women in her life gave her thousands and thousands of lessons in the fine art of communication. These ladies not only modeled how to talk and emotionally connect; they practiced connecting with her over and over. She was in a daily seminar from birth until she married, and she earned a doctorate in conversational intimacy.

Two women having a conversation create an incredible sight to behold. They fill the air with words, talk at the same time, laugh at the same time, and don't even seem to take a breath. They effortlessly reflect back to each other the content and emotions of the conversation. They give empathy and compassion without even thinking about it. They connect.

How the Wife Kills Intimacy

While the man is busy avoiding intimacy (more on this in chapter 6), the woman is hard at work accidentally killing intimacy. She's geared to go after closeness in relationships, so she tends to be too intense with her husband. She tries too hard to get close, and when she can't get connected, her powerful reaction drives the man further away.

The woman's mistakes prevent the deeper communication and emotional intimacy she so desperately wants. She turns her man away from conversation, from romance, and from treating her the way she wants to be treated.

Here are some common ways a wife kills intimacy.

The nag

You are way too aggressive in your attempts to get your husband to open up and talk personally. In your drive to get some intimacy with your man, you are too direct and apply too much pressure. You pepper him with questions. You press him for responses. You want him to tell you what he thinks and how he feels, and you want him to do it now. You bring up the same topic over and over, hoping that he'll finally talk about it. You follow him down the hall.

You are a nag, and without realizing it, you are killing conversations and robbing yourself of the intimacy you long for. Your actions are more like involuntary manslaughter because you do not intend to do this. You continually back your man into conversational corners. He feels threatened and controlled, so he will not give you the dialogue you want. He'll clam up and say nothing, snap at you in anger and frustration, or leave the room. Sound familiar?

Your style of trying to force your husband to talk turns the attempt into a complete failure. You succeed only in shutting him up and driving him further away from you. He thinks you're attacking his manhood and independence. And guess what? He's right. Your intensity becomes the only issue in his mind. As he fends off your high-pressure approach, all he's thinking is, "What a nag! What's her problem? I wish she'd back off! I just want to get away from this screaming meanie!"

She who is always right.

When you get emotional and upset, you have a tendency to think you're right. You feel very strongly about the issue, and your emotional intensity can carry you to a place where you feel morally and intellectually superior. You focus only on your opinion and your feelings.

You often don't want to hear your husband's opinion unless he agrees with you. If he disagrees, you get even more agitated and launch into a combination of lecture and finger-pointing.

I can't tell you how many men—actually, it's 52,134—who have told me privately, "Dave, I'm always wrong. Whenever she gets angry or hurt, no matter what has happened, I'm wrong. She doesn't want to hear my point of view." (This is strange, because the wives are desperate to know how their husbands feel.)

This bumper sticker says it all: "If a man was talking in a forest and no woman was there to hear him, would he still be wrong?"

The woman who talks too much.

There's just no delicate way to say it: You talk too much. You fill the air with words, tossing topic after topic at your poor man. You don't pause. You just keep going. You think conversation with your husband is like throwing spaghetti against the wall. Sooner or later, something has to stick. I mean, one of your topics has to arouse his interest. He has to respond to something you say!

No, actually he doesn't. And he won't. He simply can't process all the sentences and paragraphs gushing from your mouth. Your waves of words overwhelm his tiny brain, and his brain will explode. He shuts down. He gets distracted. He tunes you out. He goes into a different zone, staring into the distance with no expression on his face. You notice you've lost him, you get upset, and the conversation is over.

Actually a conversation never happened in the first place. It was just you talking.

During those infrequent times when he does speak, you don't let him finish. You interrupt him. You ask too many questions. You ask for more details. You want him to clarify statements. You make too many observations. You cut in and ask him to share his emotional reaction to the events he's describing: "But, honey, how did that make you *feel*?"

You're driving him crazy, and most importantly, you're choking off any possibility he'll keep talking and maybe even go a little deeper. Your interruptions make him lose his train of thought. He can focus on only one topic at a time. He simply cannot follow all the different ideas, interruptions, and rabbit trails you're throwing at him.

You think you're giving him multiple opportunities to respond. In reality, you are burying him alive with a torrent of words. His brain circuits are overloaded, he gets frustrated, and he stops talking.

Talk to me—right now!

You have a bad habit of expecting your man to respond immediately to your conversational offerings. You want to know what he's thinking and feeling about what you're talking about, and you want to know *right now*. The truth is, your man cannot give you a personal response that quickly.

You're convinced he knows what he's thinking and feeling about the topic and is simply keeping it to himself. The nerve! The utter gall of the man! Why would he be holding out on you? I'll tell you why. Because he has no idea what he's thinking and feeling. At least, not yet. He needs time to consider what you're saying and develop his personal reaction.

First, his brain moves a lot slower than yours does in the area of deeper, more personal sharing. Second, he is not in constant contact with his emotions (as you are with yours), so he needs to dig down and find them. Third, unlike you, he does not discover his emotions as he talks out loud in conversation. For him, locating emotions is a very private, internal matter. And, as I will discuss in chapter 6, the man has deliberately not expressed emotions throughout his life.

The bottom line is this: Your man needs time and space to process what you're saying so he can figure out his personal reaction to it and decide if it is safe to express it.

When you ask him to tell you about his emotions, which you have every right to do, he literally can't answer right then. He has no clue how he's feeling yet.

He'll have a delayed reaction to just about every request for his emotions. He may be able to find some feelings about the topic thirty minutes later, a few hours later, or a few days later. If you press him to identify his emotions on the spot, he'll shut down and stop talking. And that will be your fault, not his.

Your timing is terrible.

I know you and your husband can never seem to find a good time to have a deeper, more personal talk. He is famous for coming up with all kinds of excuses for why "this isn't a good time to talk." Believe me, I'm aware of all the male tricks to weasel out of conversation. I've used them all myself. But you should be aware of some very bad times to try to engage your man in deeper conversation.

Don't try to talk with him when he's hungry. His need for food is all he can think about: "Starving...Getting weaker...Must...have...sustenance...or...can't...go...on." I know this is pathetic, but that's the way it is. A man has enough trouble talking on a full stomach. If his stomach is empty, he doesn't have a chance.

Don't try to talk with him when he's tired. Talking with you requires a great deal of energy, and when he is physically and mentally fatigued, he simply doesn't have the capacity to do it. He's not asleep yet, but his brain waves are pretty slow. His system is gradually shutting down. He can watch television, feed his face with a snack, and give one- or two-word answers to simple questions. But he certainly cannot engage in a personal, meaningful conversation. You need to catch him before this shutdown process begins in the evening.

Don't try to talk to your husband when he's in bed. He may be too tired to talk (see above paragraph). Or, even worse, he'll be in an amorous mood and move into the touching mode. "Woman... in... nightgown... Been... a... couple... of... days... Must... have... sex." For a man, the bed is for sleeping and for sex. Not for talking.

Don't try to talk with him when he's just arrived home from work. He is stressed, preoccupied, and trying to make the transition from work to home, as you probably are when you come home from work too. He needs at least thirty minutes to change clothes, relax a little, and unwind from the day's headaches.

Don't try to talk with him when he's doing any other activity: watching television, reading the paper, using the computer, searching for food in the fridge, and so on. Your basic male can do only one thing at a time. He is easily distracted. Talking with you will require his total attention and concentration.

The Dialogue

Wife: What do you mean, I talk too much?

Me: It's not that you talk too much. It's that you talk too much for your man. Another woman could listen to you for hours. His attention span isn't that long. Twenty to thirty minutes at a sitting is his limit.

Wife: My husband says I ask him too many questions.

Me: He's right. You're the queen of interrogation. You're overwhelming him. You press for too much information too soon. "What about this? "What about that? "What are you thinking about right now?" Stop pumping him! He feels as if he's being given the third degree with a bright light in his face. You're going to have to limit your number of questions.

Wife: The one thing I want and need more than anything else is for him to tell me what he's thinking and feeling. You know, personal stuff. He knows I need this kind of sharing, but he refuses to do it. He deliberately clams up even though he sees how it hurts me.

Me: He doesn't open up and share because he feels pressured and because he doesn't know what he's thinking and feeling. If you keep pressing him, he'll clam up even tighter. You need to back off and let him find out what's inside.

Wife: OK, let me see if I understand this. I can't talk too much. I can't ask too many questions. I can't think I'm right just because I'm emotional about an issue. I can't pressure him to share his feelings and his thoughts immediately. And I can't try to have a deep conversation with him when he's hungry, tired, in bed, just home from work, or doing any other activity which would distract him. So how am I supposed to talk with this man and get the closeness I need?

Me: I'm glad you asked. You have a good handle on what *not* to do. Now you need to know what you *can* do. I've developed some successful strategies that will help you build better and deeper conversations with your husband.

OK, you are halfway through this chapter. Take a break and discuss these first questions together before continuing on.

Build Your Happily-Ever-After Marriage

1. Wife, tell your husband about your childhood. How much of a talker were you? Who were the women who taught you how to talk, express your feelings, and create closeness? How did they teach you?
2. Wife, describe your mom—her personality, the time she spent with you, and how she communicated her feelings. As you grew up, what kind of marriage did your mom and dad have? How did they communicate, resolve conflicts, and show affection? Did you think your mom was disappointed in her marriage in any way? How are you like your mom?
3. Wife, answer question two again, but this time apply it to your dad.

4. Wife, tell your husband which of the five intimacy-killing mistakes you believe you have made most often. Ask him which ones he feels you are guilty of the most. Ask him to lovingly catch you using these turnoffs so you can stop doing them.

Great Conversations Are Within Your Reach

One of the most common questions I hear from wives is this: "Dave, what can I do to get my husband to open up and talk personally with me?" The heart's desire of nearly every woman is to regularly connect on a deeper level in conversation with her husband. That's why she married him. That's what she wants and needs more than almost anything else.

I always give the same two answers to this question. I say, "First, you've got to stop making the classic female mistakes in communication." Then I say, "Second, you must learn some effective communication tools if you want your husband to open up and share his personal, inside information with you."

Sandy will admit that she made these five communication mistakes. She didn't intentionally kill our intimacy, but it died all the same. Of course, I was busy killing our intimacy with my own unintentional mistakes. We worked hard to identify our mistakes, and we fixed them. So can you and your husband. Here are the communication strategies that will help you develop deeper, more meaningful conversations with your husband.

Thirty-Minute Daily Talk Times

Regularly scheduled talk times create opportunities for deeper conversations with your man. These thirty-minute talk times (which I recommend you do at least four days a week) are critical and foundational prerequisites for conversational intimacy. If a couple is going to connect in communication, they need specific, intentional, focused, no-distractions-allowed times together.

I recommend the two of you have as many daily talk times as possible. One a day is the ultimate goal. Five or even six a week would be great. My counseling experience has shown that you need at least four per week to develop deeper talks.

I believe the husband, as the leader, is responsible to make sure these talk times happen each week. However, usually the wife must be the first to bring up this strategy. Perhaps a bit down the road the husband will step up and take the lead in this area.

Sit down with your husband when the kids aren't around and you aren't distracted, and present your case with words like these:

> Honey, it's very important to me that we spend regular time together in conversation. I think it's also important for us and our relationship. Our usual hit-or-miss, "talk when we get a chance" style is keeping us from the kind of closeness I think we need. I don't want to settle for an OK marriage. I want a great marriage, and talking more during the week will help us get there.

I'd like to have a thirty-minute talk time every day of the week. This may be a little unrealistic, so let's shoot for seven days but get at least four or five. Every Saturday or Sunday, let's sit down and schedule our talk times for the upcoming week. We'll select the four or five days that look the best for us. We'll put these appointments on the calendar, in our Day-Timers, and in our smart phones.

We need to enjoy our talk times in a quiet, comfortable, and private place at home. We can't allow any distractions. No television, no kids, no pets, no phones, no magazines or newspapers, and no computer. Just the two of us alone.

These four or five talk times will help me stop nagging and pressuring you to talk. I won't have to talk your head off, as I do now during those few times during the week when I try to get your attention. I'll be able to relax and save most of my talking for these specific times. We'll be closer, and I'll be happier. I really think this will make me more interested in sex and more responsive in bed. (This last part will definitely get his attention.)

Once we have selected the days we'll have a talk time, I'd like us to post a talk-time schedule for that week. Let's say we choose Monday, Wednesday, Thursday, and Friday. We'll write these days on a piece of paper with a column under each day. If we have a topic we'd like to discuss on a certain day, we jot it down in the column under that day. For example, if I want to talk about the pastor's

> sermon during our Monday talk time, I'd jot that topic in the Monday column.
>
> This system will not only help us remember what we want to talk about but also be a good way to continue talking about certain topics. For example, if either of us wants to continue to talk about the pastor's sermon after Monday, we can write that topic in the Wednesday column. If one of us wants to talk about the sermon again, we can write it in the Thursday column. Let's post this talk-time schedule someplace where we'll both see it every day, like the refrigerator, the kitchen door, or the big mirror in our bedroom.

After asking your husband for his response and getting his input on the regular talk times and the posted schedule, ask him to pray with you about it. After the prayer, ask him to think and pray about these ideas for two or three days. Set a day and time to come back together to discuss these strategies and make some decisions. At this second meeting, assuming he is willing to try these strategies, the two of you will schedule your first four talk times and post your talk-time schedule.

These foundational communication strategies will create real intimacy by allowing you to apply the carry-over principle, which says that to achieve depth in conversation, a woman and a man must talk about the same topic two, three, or even four times. Each time you talk about the topic, you get a little deeper.

The man cannot express his personal thoughts and feelings about a topic in the first conversation about it.

He needs time to process and figure out what's inside. With this system, he can process and revisit the topic in the next two or three scheduled talk times. Rather than dying an early and untimely death, a topic can live on into the next few talk times.

It's Time to Talk Smart

Wife, you consistently make two major mistakes when you're talking with your man. (I have already discussed these mistakes, but they are so important I must repeat them.) First, you use too many words and overwhelm his limited attention span. He has attention deficit disorder when you talk too much. He just can't take it!

When you rattle on too long—which means anything over five minutes—even a man with decent listening skills can't hang in there with you. As you drone on, here's what he's thinking:

- What was point number eight?
- I'm drowning in her ocean of details.
- Please, get to the point.
- I'm begging you, move on.
- Stop beating a dead horse!
- Stop the torture! I give up! I'll tell you where the important papers are!
- Lord, please come now and rescue me from this agony.

Your man will lose his concentration. He won't be able to focus. He'll get overloaded. He'll tune you out. When he tunes you out, you'll catch him as you always do, and the conversation will be over. You'll be angry and hurt, he'll be a dirt ball who doesn't care about you, and life will stink.

Your second mistake is expecting him to be able to respond immediately to what you're saying. You want his personal thoughts, emotions, and reactions, and you want them right now. You fail to realize that your man has a very slow processor. He needs time, from two hours to two days or more, to study what you've said and figure out a personal response.

These two mistakes are killing the majority of your conversations with your man. You need to talk smart with him, and I have a strategy that will help you do that. I call it one-way communication.

One-Way Communication

In one-way communication, you briefly tell your man your view, your thoughts, and your emotions about a topic and do not expect an immediate reply. I call it one-way because you do all the talking.

You tell him he doesn't have to respond. You ask him to listen and concentrate in order to understand, to take time to process what you've said, and then, when he's ready, to share his reaction. When you're done talking, you either walk away or simply go silent. If you're with him at home in a couple's talk time, in the car, in a restaurant, or out somewhere, just be quiet for at least five minutes. After the five minutes, you can bring up another topic of conversation.

You speak your piece and move on. Unlike what you've done in the past, you do not press him for an immediate reaction. Why not? Two reasons: First, men cannot respond right away. They need time to process and figure out their feelings and thoughts on an issue. Personal issues require even more time. Second, men will always clam up when they feel pressured by women. They feel controlled, and they demonstrate with their silence that no one can make them talk.

If you express yourself in five minutes or fewer and allow him time to process, you increase the likelihood that your man will consider what you say and get back to you to continue the conversation. If you nag him or even ask him sweetly for a quick response, your man will harden up and never respond on that topic. Never. My way, the one-way communication strategy, gets you a maybe. Your way, the natural female way of pushing him to say something right away, gets you a never. Try it my way.

You can try several different types of one-way communication. Let's take a look at them.

The five-minute burst during talk time

For regular, no-conflict talk times, try the five-minute one-way burst. As you begin speaking, ask him right up front to listen and reflect back to you what he hears. As you talk, check in with him periodically to make sure he's engaged with you: "Are you with me, honey?" "Do you understand what I'm saying?" "What emotion do you think I'm feeling right now?" You're not asking for his response to what you're saying. You're seeing if he understands the basic content and your emotions.

Talk for five minutes, and then stop. Give him a chance to think, to digest what you've said, and to prepare some kind of a response. He might say something back, or he might not. At least by pausing, you've given him an opportunity to connect with you.

If he says nothing during your pause, let five minutes go by. Don't jump right back in with more comments on the same topic. After your five-minute pause, talk about another topic for five minutes, and pause again. If he doesn't respond, let ten minutes go by. By being silent more often, you might motivate him to initiate more conversations. He'll notice your silence and may talk more to draw you back closer to him.

At the end of your thirty-minute talk time, tell him the one or two topics you'd like him to process and about which to get back to you. Tell him you'll jot these topics on the talk-time schedule under the day of your next meeting. Or tell him he can do it. This is the best way to remind him you want to hear what he has to say on these topics.

The five-minute burst at other times

Obviously you and your man will talk outside of the four or five talk times you schedule each week. In these times, make sure you have his full attention. Then talk for five minutes or fewer about a topic. Tell him you'd like him to think about what you've said and get back to you with his response when he's ready. Tell him he can respond before your next scheduled talk time (you should be so lucky!) or he can wait until the talk time. Go ahead and jot the topic on the talk-time schedule under the day of your next meeting. If he happens to respond before the meeting (miracles do happen!), you can just cross that item off the talk-time schedule.

The thirty-second burst when he fails to respond

What if you use one-way communication and he still doesn't come back to you with a response? Well, he is a man, and that's certainly going to happen a lot. When you've waited a day or two and you see he clearly has no intention of giving you a response, take two steps.

Step one is to give him a low-key, no-emotion reminder. You are allowed only one. If you remind him twice, you're a nag. In thirty seconds or fewer, say something like this: "Remember that issue we discussed? When you're ready, I'd like you to find me and give me your reaction to what I said." You could also add, "I'll put this topic on the talk-time schedule for our next meeting." After these statements, say nothing else about it. Move on.

If he still won't talk about it, go to step two. Go to him and give him a one-way communication that expresses your feelings about his decision to ignore you and refuse to respond to the topic. Say something like this: "I'm angry and disappointed that you've chosen to not come back to me about [whatever issue you brought up]. That makes me feel unloved and unimportant. I just wanted you to know." Then drop it and walk away. Don't bring it up again.

This cleans your system of anger and resentment, allows you to forgive him, and gives you closure on the issue. And just maybe he will feel bad and come back to you with a response to the issue.

The thirty-second burst when he doesn't want to talk

He's obviously upset about something. You ask him a reasonable question: "What's wrong?" He says, "Nothing." Instead of yelling, "Liar!" give him a thirty-second one-way burst with words like these: "Look, I know something's wrong. I know it's hard for you to talk about it, so I won't try to pry it out of you. I want to comfort and support you, but I can't if you don't tell me what's bothering you. When you want to share what it is, come to me. You can share it a little at a time over several days, and I'll just listen and reflect back to you what I'm hearing."

The thirty-second burst in response to his male shtick

Until now, your responses to your husband's male behaviors have been ineffective. When he's killed conversation after conversation with his standard maneuvers to avoid intimacy, you've cried, yelled, lectured, whispered, begged, pleaded, reasoned, threatened, and ignored. Nothing has worked. He's still not talking, and you're still a wife with no intimacy.

Time to try something new, something that has a much better chance of working. I want you to respond to his classic male communication-killing shtick with brief verbal surgical strikes. The choreographed one-way responses I've included below will rattle your man and create some real changes in your relationship. But these snappy comebacks will also keep you sane and give you some fun. When you live with a man, you need some entertainment.

Husband: *[He's not listening to you. His eyes are glazed over. He's in the "zone."]*

Wife: Brain cramp, huh? I'm insulted and angry because you're not paying attention to me. If you don't want to listen to me, say so. Let me know when you're ready to listen. *[Stop talking and make him come to you to restart the conversation.]*

Husband: *[He falls silent as you talk. He gives no responses at all.]*

Wife: You're not saying anything. I can't tell if you're listening. If you don't want to talk about this, tell me. If you're OK with this topic, give me some responses so I know you're with me. It's frustrating to talk and get no feedback, so I won't do it. I'll wait for you to tell me what's on your mind.

Husband: *[He's not completely shut down, but his mind is somewhere else. He's giving you one- and two-word answers.]*

Wife: You seem out of it tonight. You're not involved in this conversation. I won't keep trying to get you interested in me and what I'm saying. If I do, I'll get angry, and so will you. Come to me when you're ready to talk. I'd like to know what you're thinking about tonight, but you'll have to decide to tell me.

Husband: *[He drops one of his logical conversation-killer comments on you.]* You shouldn't feel that way. You're way too intense. You're overreacting. Simmer down, and I'll show you the facts. You're wrong, and I can prove it. Here's how to fix your problem.

Wife: Hold it right there. I don't need logic. I'm not going to listen to it now. If I did, I'd get furious. What I need now is for you to listen to me, reflect back to me what I'm saying, and help me feel understood. When you're ready to do that, let me know. Once I feel understood, I'll be happy to listen to your logic.

Husband: *[You've asked him, "How was your day?"]* Fine. *[Or]* OK.

Wife: That one word really doesn't tell me too much. I need more information than that. Take some time and think about your day, and then find me and tell me what you come up with.

Husband: I don't know.

Wife: When you do know, come and find me and tell me. We can't build a conversation on "I don't know."

Husband: I don't want to talk about it.

Wife: OK. I respect that. Please listen to me talk about it for five minutes. Hear me out. You don't have to give me your view now. After you think about what I've said and you're ready to talk, find me. Or you can wait until our next talk time.

Husband: This isn't a good time to talk about it.

Wife: What if I tell you "This isn't a good time" the next time you want sex? What sex is to you, communication is to me. When you're ready to talk about this, find me, and we'll schedule a meeting.

Is this approach a little edgy? Yes. Will it be unnerving to your man? Yes. Will it make you a challenge for him? Yes. Will it shake him out of his no-personal-sharing comfort zone and motivate him to pursue you and talk more? Quite possibly.

These responses may seem manipulative, but they are not. They are honest statements that communicate your feelings and have a good chance of motivating him to open up and talk.

When He Talks

When your man talks, let him talk and don't interrupt him. Don't ask him a bunch of questions. Don't jump ahead and make comments about where you think he's headed in the story. Don't bring up topics his story triggers in your mind. Don't press him for his emotional reaction.

OK, that's what you don't do. Here's what you do. Let him be logical during the first part of the conversation. He's a logical creature, so he'll start with the facts and events only. Your job is to listen and reflect. By *reflect,* I mean briefly say back to him the content (the facts and his thoughts) and the emotion (his feelings about what he is saying).

Be very low-key when you reflect his emotions. Wait until he's expressed at least a few paragraphs, and then tell him how you think he's feeling: "I'll bet that made you feel..." Just mention a few emotions, and don't ask him to confirm your guesses or comment further on his emotional state. This strategy will help him identify his emotions and give him a head start on his processing.

After reflecting what he's said and how you think he's feeling, you can ask him a few questions (two or three at most). Ask him to take some time to process and get back to you with his responses. Tell him you'd like to continue the talk on his topic when he's ready. One of you can put the topic on the talk-time schedule.

Let Him Pursue You

Stop chasing him. Stop using a direct, in-your-face approach to get him to talk. Stop pressuring him to talk. Stop nagging him to talk. Stop pouting and whining, hoping he'll feel guilty and talk. Stop talking too much.

All these behaviors put you in pursuit of him. That is not God's design for you, so it will never work. He is the leader who is to pursue you with the same kind of love Christ has for the church (Eph. 5:22–26).

If you pursue him, he will feel cornered and controlled and defensive. As a result, his walls will go way up and he won't talk.

The strategies in this chapter work because they jibe with the way a man communicates. They also work on a deeper level because they consistently make him the pursuer and you the pursued. If you can get him to pursue you, you will change your entire communication system. A man will communicate more deeply and personally when he's in pursuit of his woman.

Build Your Happily-Ever-After Marriage

1. How often during the average week do the two of you have times to talk that you have planned and scheduled? What has kept you from having talks like these?
2. Are you willing to follow the strategy of scheduling at least four talk times a week? Right now, schedule your first four.
3. How will the act of posting your talk-time schedule improve the depth of your communication as a couple? Where will you post this schedule?
4. Wife, how do you feel about the one-way communication strategy? Husband, how do you feel about it? Which type of one-way communication will be the hardest to do? Which type do you think will help your communication as a couple the most?
5. Husband, tell your wife what she can be doing when you're talking that will help you communicate more deeply and personally. What strategy could she follow that would help you the most?
6. Who is the communication pursuer in your relationship? Wife, if it's you, are you willing to give up that role? Husband, are you willing to pursue her? How will you do that?

Chapter Six

MISTAKE #4: HUSBAND, YOU'RE AVOIDING INTIMACY

Take the Lead, Listen Smart, and Share Personally

THE WIFE HAS taken her medicine. We have exposed her mistakes in communication and discussed the solutions. But I've told only half the story about communication.

Husband, as they used to say in biblical days, it's time to "gird up your loins." In other words, hunker down. Batten down the hatches. You're in for a rough ride. It's your turn in the hot seat. You, sir, are also making communication mistakes. And these mistakes are limiting the intimacy in your marriage. You need to change.

So, let's get to it.

Men Are Born Doers

God created William, our son. And then there was destruction. And there was yelling, running, climbing, wild laughter, and loud animal noises. And constant activity.

Seven-year-old William, like most boys—and men—is a doer. From the moment he gets up at the crack of dawn (he's slept in an extra hour exactly twice in his first seven years) to the moment he finally goes to sleep at night, William is doing something. He plays video games and computer games, engages in every outdoor sport he can with his neighborhood buddies, rides his bike, swims in the pool, plays board games and card games, and bugs his sisters. If he watches a movie, it had better be sports oriented or filled with nonstop, dramatic action.

William does talk, but only about four things: what he's done, what he's doing right now, what he's going to do, and sports. If he's not doing something, he's miserable. He can't stand just sitting around and talking. He hates chick movies. He's not sensitive. His sisters' feelings aren't on his radar. He just wants to play, play, play and do, do, do.

Like most males, William is a doer because he has a God-given need to compete with others and maintain control in relationships. If William is going to be a good husband someday, he will have to learn to open up and communicate with a woman. Sandy and I are trying to teach him these skills, but we face an uphill battle. It's against his nature, and he just doesn't get it...yet.

William has no desire to get in touch with his feelings. Even if—by some miracle—he did identify his feelings, he'd rather take a beating than express them to another person. Especially to a girl. He doesn't cry very often. That's for wimps and mamas' boys. He feels close to someone when they do something together.

Raised to Avoid Closeness

Your typical man isn't just born to avoid intimacy. He's also raised to avoid it. Watching his parents and their relationship taught him all he needed to know about sidestepping closeness.

His dad was probably another intimacy avoider. Just as a master craftsman teaches his apprentice, his dad likely taught him the proud, honorable trade of holding in feelings and being a poor communicator. Through years and years of modeling, he has been carefully trained to carry on the family business of building a mediocre marriage.

He probably never, and I mean *never*, saw a significant man in his life share something personal. It just didn't happen. Dad didn't do it. Neither of his grandpas did it. His brother didn't do it. Uncle Harry didn't do it. None of his male teachers or coaches did it. He learned *not* to share personal things with other men, and certainly not with women.

What he did see, time after time until there were too many times to count, was his dad and other key men in his life choking back their emotions. Stuffing all personal reactions. Refusing to answer personal questions women asked. Saying as little as possible and sticking to the facts. Being logical. Avoiding conflicts. Showing emotions only while watching sports.

He may also have seen his mom and dad develop and maintain a marriage devoid of any real intimacy. It may have been a decent marriage but not a great one. He saw his mom carry on bravely for years, enabling her husband and acting as though everything was OK with her. In truth, she was unhappy and unfulfilled. But he didn't see his mom's pain.

He thought—and still thinks—his parent's marriage was "fine" or "OK." He actually believes the relationship they had (and may still have) is as good as marriage gets. He'll say, "They had a good marriage." "They got along." "They never fought." "They built a solid, stable life together." Wonderful. Doesn't sound too exciting or passionate, does it? If his parents got divorced or had some obvious trouble in their marriage, he has no idea why.

No wonder a man can't emotionally connect. All the men in his growing-up years modeled poor communication. He's never seen a man and a woman engage in personal, deep conversation. He's never experienced emotional intimacy with another person. He has no idea what intimacy looks like. He has no idea how to get it. All he knows is how to avoid intimacy. He has those skills down cold because he was trained by the best.

How the Husband Avoids Emotional Intimacy

The vast majority of men were born and raised to avoid intimacy with other persons. They're clueless about closeness. They're uncomfortable with deep, personal conversations. They're geared to get away from any interaction that might lead to emotional connection.

The man is a master of avoiding intimacy. He's been doing it his whole life. Like the Great Houdini, he is a world-class escape artist. He'll do whatever is necessary to weasel out of a close, deep conversation with his wife.

Here are some of his escape-from-closeness tricks.

Answering a question with a question

Your wife asks you, "How are you doing?" You respond, "Why do you ask?" She's thinking, "What do you mean, Why do I ask? I'm trying to start a conversation. I want to know you better."

She asks you, "What are you thinking?" You respond with a question that makes no sense: "Who knows?" Your wife is thinking, "Well, I guess the only person who knows would be you."

Pleading ignorance

Here is one of your classic escape lines to any question requiring personal information: "I don't know." It's a beautiful, inoffensive way to kill a conversation cold. You're really telling your woman, "I'd love to talk to you, honey, but I have no information. If only I could think of one thing that happened to me today…but I can't. Sorry. My mind's a complete blank." It's amazing how a man knows completely zilch when his wife is trying to get a conversation going. The fact is that you just don't want to talk, and this brain freeze is a wonderful excuse.

Massive generalizations

Your wife asks, "How was your day?" You answer "Fine" or "OK." Too bad you can't build much of a conversation on these two global replies.

Of course, that's why you respond this way. You want to give her nothing to work with. You have nicely answered her question and escaped any possibility of closeness. This is like her asking, "Where do you live?" and you responding, "The universe."

No response

You simply don't respond to her questions. You say absolutely nothing. Like a statue in a park, your face and body are carved out of stone. Your wife could spray you with whipped cream—and it's tempting—and you'd give no reaction. She's thinking, "Am I here? Does he see me? Did he hear me?" Oh, you heard all right. You're exercising elective mutism. You're letting her know you don't want to talk about whatever topic she has brought up.

Refusal to talk

"I don't want to talk about it." How many times have you told your wife that? Or its corollary, "This isn't a good time to talk"? You're too tired, stressed, and preoccupied with the television. It's time to go to bed, you have to check the e-mail, etc. You seem to indicate that someday, somewhere, you will find a good time to talk. Believe me, your wife won't live that long.

Letting her talk all the time

You're usually happy to let your woman talk. Of course, not that you're always listening that closely. If she's talking and filling the air with words, you don't have to talk.

A monologue does not create intimacy. Since intimacy requires a dialogue, you avoid it by encouraging her to ramble on alone.

Snap and then leave

You get angry, snap some nasty comment at her, and leave the room. You simply can't stand up and leave, so you create a reason to get out of the conversation. You don't want to leave (yeah, sure), but she made you angry, so you have to go. If she gets angry or exasperated, which would be perfectly understandable, that plays right into your hands. You'll say she's overreacting, and since you can't talk to an overreactor, you have to leave. And it's her fault!

Drop it and move on

When she wants to talk through a conflict, you accuse her of dwelling on the past. You fail to recognize that the past is not the past until you've dealt with it together and come to an understanding. You use statements like, "I said I was sorry," or, "Stop bringing that up" to end conflict conversations. You believe if she drops the subject, the problem will magically disappear.

Like most husbands, you absolutely hate conflict with your wife. You'd rather face a firing squad than work through a conflict with her. Dealing with conflict, for you, is like turning the car around, going back two miles, scraping roadkill from the pavement, and eating it for dinner.

You don't understand that if you ignore or sidestep a conflict, it doesn't go away. It remains, festers, and pushes the two of you further apart. Unintentionally you are hurting and disrespecting your wife. The unresolved conflict also carries over to the next conflict, so when you fight over the next thing, you're fighting about the current issue *and* all the other unresolved conflicts. You see, you can't just drop it and move on. You'll drag it along behind you.

Too busy to talk

You're a busy man. You've got to do a lot of important things, and, sad though it is, that just doesn't leave any time to talk with her. You have to work, watch television, dink around on the computer, do yard work, fix things around the house, read the paper, sleep, or whatever else you can think of to avoid conversation with her.

You're more comfortable doing activities that you enjoy, that help you escape from stress, and that you're good at doing. Talking with your wife is tough, and you don't feel very competent in this area. So you wimp out of it by staying busy doing things you'd rather do. You're not fooling her. You're breaking her heart.

Can't talk but can have sex

She starts talking, and you start fondling her. She's trying to connect emotionally, and her conversationally impaired husband is in touching mode! Why waste time talking when you can have sex? When she doesn't respond favorably (what a shocker!), you get offended and accuse her of rejecting you. You're angry and pouty, so, of course, no one would expect you to talk to her.

You don't realize that her need for emotional connection is just as powerful as your need for sex. And because she cannot respond sexually *without* the emotional connection, you must learn to talk with her and meet her emotional needs *before* sex.

The logical man

You bury your emotions and are aware only of cold, hard, rational logic. When your wife expresses her emotions, you don't realize she is being a normal and healthy female, a fully functional human being. You see her expression as bizarre, unnecessary, and frightening. You try your logic to talk her out of her feelings: "Honey, you shouldn't feel that way." "Honey, calm down, and let's look at the facts." "Honey, listen up, and I'll tell you how to fix your problem." Of course, your logic infuriates her and hurts her. Conversation over.

Haven't you noticed how many conversations you kill with your logic? Your wife is emotional and expressing herself about a topic. You come back with a logical response. She gets even more emotional and intense because she needs understanding, not logic. You get frustrated and edgy and defensive because you don't want her to be more emotional. Then...

This is not going to end well. You and your wife will not connect in this conversation. And now you get the added bonus of a woman who is upset. Hurt. Angry.

Unhappy. You will now pay the price for your logical responses. And it's your own fault.

The martyr

When your wife urges you to talk, you say in a whiny, pitiful voice, "I guess I can't ever please you." Somehow, your refusal to talk becomes your wife's fault because she can't be pleased. You think her expectations are too high. You think she wants too much. You are a poor, well-meaning man who has tried his best, and your best is just not good enough for her.

This clever ruse is nothing more than a distraction from the real issue. Your wife's expectation that you share yourselves and your lives is reasonable. She wants what every wife wants!

The genetic excuse

If all else fails, you will resort to these old standards: "Hey, this who I am." "You knew I was like this when you chose to marry me." "I can't change." Bogus, bogus, bogus. This may be who you are, but you don't have to stay that way. Unless you both were frozen solid right after your wedding and put into cold storage, you both need to change as the marriage progresses. You *can* change, and you *need* to change if the two of you are going to build an intimate relationship. When people refuse to change, they almost never have wonderful marriages. In fact, their marriages often don't survive. But God is in the business of changing believers' lives.

The Dialogue

Husband: Doc, she wants to talk all the time. She's always asking me questions.

Me: I know. You married a woman. She really wants to know who you are, to be close to you. Don't fight her. Let her in!

Husband: I'm a simple guy. All I need is food on the table, sex on a regular basis, and peace at home.

Me: Spoken like a true man. But your wife needs more than these basic things. Frankly, even though you don't realize it yet, so do you. You both have a God-given need for the emotional connection that comes through deeper conversations.

Husband: I don't talk much. I don't have much to say. You might say I'm a man of few words.

Me: Yeah, your wife has noticed. Look, you don't have to become some huge talker. You just have to learn to talk and share *enough*. She'll be happy with that.

Husband: When she's upset and emotional, I try to calm her down. But she gets more upset!

Me: Ever throw gasoline on a fire? That's what you're doing when you use logic to help her calm down. She doesn't need logic. She needs you to listen, to reflect back to her what you are hearing, and to give her understanding.

Husband: I have no idea how to communicate with her. Nobody ever taught me how to do it.

Me: That's where I come in. I'm going to teach you how. My strategies have worked for thousands of husbands in my therapy office and in my marriage seminars. They'll work for you too.

This is a good place to pause and discuss what's been covered so far.

Build Your Happily-Ever-After Marriage

1. Husband, tell your wife about your childhood. How active were you as a boy? In what activities did you participate? Were you a doer or a talker?
2. Husband, describe your dad—his personality, the time he spent with you, and the way he communicated his feelings. What kind of marriage did your dad and mom have as you grew up? How did they communicate, resolve conflicts, and show affection? How are you like your dad?
3. Husband, answer question two again, but this time apply it to your mom.
4. Husband, tell your wife which of the thirteen escape–from-closeness tricks you believe you use most often. Ask her which ones you use the most. Ask her to lovingly

catch you using these tricks so you can stop doing them.

Good-Bye, Great Houdini; Hello, Good Communicator

Does anything in this chapter sound familiar? I'll bet it does. I was guilty of all these communication mistakes with Sandy. That's why I can describe them so well.

For the first ten years of our marriage, I didn't have a clue about how to communicate with my wife. I had to realize that all my intimacy-avoidance techniques were hurting me, Sandy, and our relationship. I wasn't intentionally causing damage and pain. Sidestepping closeness was automatic for me. It's what came naturally. I had no idea I was keeping us from an intimate, joyful life together.

But I figured out what I was doing wrong, and with help from God and Sandy, I made the necessary corrections. I still make mistakes, but most of the time I do things right. And that has made all the difference in our communication and in our marriage.

If I can do it, you can do it. Let's get to the how-tos.

You Are the Man

I'll get right to the point. It's your job to lead the way to better communication. In fact, it's your job to lead your wife in every area of your relationship. I'm not telling you that, God is:

> Wives, be submissive to your own husbands as unto the Lord. For the husband is the head of the wife, just as Christ is the head and Savior of the church, which is His body. But as the church submits to Christ, so also let the wives be to their own husbands in everything.
>
> —Ephesians 5:22–24

Pretty clear, isn't it? God didn't leave any loopholes when assigning leadership in marriage. If the wife leads in communication, it will never be efficient or successful. It can't be! Female leadership is not God's design. Both of you are to be involved in the communication process, but God wants *you* to lead the way.

Your first duty as communication leader is to create regular times to talk and make sure you have topics to discuss. Remember the thirty-minute daily talk times and the talk-time schedule from chapter 5? If you haven't read that chapter, read it right now. You need the information. Go ahead. Your wife will wait.

Husband, you are responsible to sit down with your wife and schedule at least four thirty-minute talk times each week. You are responsible to go to her and say, "It's time for our talk, honey." You are also responsible to post the talk-time schedule and ensure you are using it properly.

You noticed in chapter 5 that your wife may approach you and seek to establish the talk times and talk-time schedule. Very often, the wife has to initially take the lead because the husband won't. Don't force your wife to do it. That is definitely Plan B. In Plan A, God's plan, you step up and get the job done.

What Do We Talk About?

Husband, you're also in charge of what happens during your talk times. I don't mean you'll be the one doing all the talking. Both you and your wife will talk, and you will listen. But you will guide the content and flow of the talk times. In other words, as the CEO here, you run the meeting and determine the agenda.

Here's your crash course in how to run a couple's talk time.

Step 1: Create some ambiance

Meet with your wife in an atmosphere that is warm, soft, and inviting. This is more important to her than it is to you. Make sure the conversation area is clear of empty cups, wrappers, and miscellaneous clutter. Have some low-key music playing in the background, like one of her favorite worship or other Christian CDs. Get her a cup of coffee, a mug of tea, or a soft drink. Burning one or two candles wouldn't be a bad idea. Offer to give her a neck, back, or foot massage as you sit down and begin the meeting.

Step 2: Offer a brief prayer

Take her hand and say a short prayer. It could be something like this: "Dear Father, Thank You for my wonderful wife. Thank You for this time we have together. Please be with us and help us open up and really connect in conversation." This will automatically deepen the mood and help you both prepare to communicate.

Step 3: Read a devotional

When you're just starting your talk times, coming up with conversational material can be difficult. An easy and effective way to kick off communication is to read a page from a couples' devotional book and answer the questions at the end of the page. My two favorite devotionals for couples are Dr. James and Shirley Dobson's *Night Light* and Dennis and Barbara Rainey's *Moments Together for Couples.*

Husband, prepare by reading the devotional page in advance. Being a man, you need time to digest the information and process it. Use a writing pad to jot down your comments and reactions. You may also use your iPhone or other electronic device. This way, you'll have some things to say. And she'll be impressed that you spent time preparing to talk with her.

After reading the devotional page, both of you can discuss your reactions to it and answer the questions at the end. It may trigger a stimulating conversation. Something on the page or in a question may lead to a deeper talk. If you find an interesting topic and want to talk about it again, jot it down on your pad. Think about the topic over the next day or so, and jot down your impressions and ideas. Then, at the next talk time, you can continue to talk on that topic by sharing what you have on your pad.

Your wife doesn't need a pad. She remembers everything. She'll be impressed that you did some work on the topic, and she will have no trouble jumping right into the conversation.

Step 4: Revisit carryover topics

Next, you can segue into revisiting subjects of interest you've discussed in previous talk times or in other conversations. This is the carryover principle I explained in chapter 5—talking about the same topic two, three, or four times to achieve a deeper level of emotional intimacy.

Whether you bring up one of these carryover topics or your wife does, you can say, "Yes, the pastor's sermon. We talked about that on Monday and agreed to continue that talk today. I thought more about it, and I wrote down some things that came into my head."

Without the pad, you'll sit there like the village idiot with absolutely nothing to say. "What? The sermon? Are you sure we talked about that? I forgot what the sermon was about, and I'm fuzzy on our talk about it." With the pad, you'll sit there like a man who cares enough about his wife to remember topics of conversation and actually prepare to talk more about them. You'll go from being a man who doesn't talk to a caring conversationalist. The man who doesn't talk gets disappointment, disgust, no respect, no intimacy, and mediocre sex. The caring conversationalist gets warmth, love, emotional intimacy, respect, and better and more frequent sex. So, who do you want to be?

If both of you decide to continue talking about a carryover topic, jot it on your pad and put it on the talk-time schedule.

Step 5: Discuss life events

After getting a little deeper into one or two carryover topics, you can bring up new material: work, kids, home maintenance, social plans, friends and family, church, and events of interest that have occurred since your last talk time.

If any of these prove stimulating and promise more intimacy, agree to carry them over to the next talk time. Jot these topics on your pad or electronic device for processing, and write them on the talk-time schedule.

I'll say this one more time to make sure you get it: If you agree to keep talking about any topic that comes up during your talk time, jot it *immediately* on your pad, and *immediately* put it on the talk-time schedule. Keep the talk-time schedule with you during the talk time.

Step 6: Pray together

Make a list of prayer requests on a pad. You may call this your prayer pad. Divide the list into one for each of you, and pray aloud, one at a time, for the items on your list. Make sure you hold her hand during this five-minute prayer time. If you're in a crisis or have a pressing concern, you'll pray for more than five minutes. Remember to thank God for who He is, His many blessings, and His presence and help.

Step 7: Let prayer lead to conversation

When you finish praying, you will naturally talk about some of the issues you just lifted up to God. These are the concerns of your heart, and following up on them with conversation can lead to real emotional intimacy.

Step 8: Be open

This progression I've explained is not set in concrete. It has, however, proven very helpful to many couples who are beginning the talk-time program. It provides some structure, a nice flow, and multiple opportunities for deeper conversations. Try it, and see how it goes. Play with the order of steps, and mix it up to find a sequence that works best for you and your wife. Every now and then, change the order to keep things fresh.

Conversational intimacy is unpredictable, so in every talk time the sequence of steps is subject to sudden change. If you hit a winning topic and you are building an interesting conversation, go with it. Following a potentially intimate conversational branch is more important than covering all the steps in the talk-time progression.

Now, let's go a little deeper into the specific areas of listening and talking to your woman. These principles will apply to the talk times and to conversations that occur at other times.

Listen Smart

Listening to your wife in a smart way is a critical part of good communication. If you listen in a dumb way, you'll kill the communication. She has to know that you get it, that you grasp what she's saying and feeling. This is the first essential link in the chain of conversation.

Before I explain the how-tos, here are the benefits of listening smart:

- You'll build understanding.
- She'll come down in emotional intensity.
- She'll feel closer to you.
- She'll feel loved.
- You'll get warmed up and into the conversation.
- You'll be able to share more personally.
- She'll talk less because she knows you're getting it.
- She'll be ready to listen to what you have to say.
- She'll be happy.

The consequences of listening dumb are just the opposite:

- You'll create no understanding.
- She'll go up in emotional intensity.
- She'll feel more distant from you.
- She'll feel unloved.
- You won't warm up and will stay out of the conversation.
- You won't be able to share more personally.
- She'll talk more because she knows you're not getting it.

- She won't want to listen to what you have to say.
- She'll be unhappy.

The stakes are high. Very high. You need to learn to listen smart. Here's how.

Be an active listener.

Listening smart means being an active listener. When she opens her beautiful mouth to speak, allow no distractions. Establish eye contact. Lock on her just as a missile locks on its target. As she speaks, verbally feed back her content (what she is saying) and her emotion (what you think she is feeling about what she is saying). You don't repeat everything she says; just repeat key words and phrases so she knows you understand her message, like this:

> Boy, you had a lot of fun at the beach. Except for that dumb parking attendant, you and your girlfriends had a great time. You felt relaxed and close to your friends.
>
> That nurse at the doctor's office was way out of line. I can't believe how she treated you. Talk about rude! I don't blame you for being furious.
>
> I'm sorry your dad treated you so bad. What an insensitive jerk! I can see you're angry and sad. I don't know why he can't be proud of you and all you've accomplished.

As you feed back her content and emotion, ask her periodically if she feels understood:

- "Do you feel I'm understanding what you're saying and feeling?"
- "Do you feel I'm getting it?"
- "Are you angry or more frustrated at my responses?"
- "Do you feel I'm with you in this conversation?"

You need to actively listen regardless of what your wife is saying or feeling. You must actively listen even when she's saying something you consider trivial. When she's emotionally intense. When she seems unreasonable, irrational, or isn't making any sense. When she's convinced she's right. When she jumps from topic to topic, following a whole series of conversational rabbit trails. When she changes her mind.

You need to actively listen when she repeats herself. When a woman talks, she'll repeat a story three or four times. That's the way she figures out her emotions and determines how to react to what happened to her. If you actively listen, she will talk less. But she'll still repeat herself. You must hang in there and stay in active listening mode.

Always, always, always actively listen to her first, before you say anything. Later, after she feels understood, you can share the original things you have to say, your point of view, your perspective, and your opinion.

Be captivated by her talking.

Every woman, including yours, wants her husband to be captivated by her. The deep desire of her heart is for her man to find her irresistible, fascinating, and interesting. Read these words Solomon spoke to his sweetie:

> Let me see your face,
> let me hear your voice;
> for your voice is sweet,
> and your face is lovely.
>
> —Song of Songs 2:14

Solomon wanted to hear his woman's voice. He was hanging on to her every word! He was attracted to her physical beauty and also to her conversation. The Shulammite woman was thrilled by Solomon's attention and loved him right back.

So be like Solomon and enjoy the show when your wife is talking. Her expressiveness, spontaneity, emotional intensity, and unpredictable conversational style are very entertaining. If she talked like you—logically, without many words and without much emotion—the two of you would be bored to death. Thank God every day that she is a woman and talks like a woman.

Relive her story.

Allow yourself—push yourself—to be emotionally drawn into the story she is telling. She doesn't need you to be a mere observer, standing outside and watching her tell her story. She needs you to be a participant, reliving her story right alongside her.

When she's describing an event, here's what she's thinking:

- "See what happened to me?"
- "Do you feel what I felt going through it?"
- "Do you understand what it was like for me?"
- "I want you to know me better because you walked through this experience with me."

This kind of "walk in her shoes, feel what she feels" empathy is not one of your strong points. She's a lot better at it than you are. But you can do it. When you watch an action-adventure movie, you get into the story, don't you? You feel emotions, and you can relate to the hero as he kills the bad guys, fights past the obstacles, and rescues the woman, right? Of course you do. Your challenge is to react and respond in these same ways to your wife when she's telling a story about an event in her life.

One of the key ways to relive events with your wife is to mirror her emotions as she's talking. Work hard to feel what she is feeling. Don't just become cognizant of her emotion; actually feel some of it yourself. This is Romans 12:15 in action: "Rejoice with those who rejoice, and weep with those who weep." If she's angry, you're angry. And let her see your anger. If she's sad, you're sad. If she's frustrated, you're frustrated. If she's happy, you're happy. You won't feel 100 percent of what she's feeling because you're not her. And you're not that good at empathetic listening.

Work at this, and do your best. You'll get better at it with practice.

Another way to relive her events and feel connected to her is to ask specific questions about the details of her story. This shows interest and helps draw you into her story. Zero in on the aspects of her story that interest you, and ask questions:

- "What did you say when the parking guy spit on the ground?"
- "What did that nurse look like?"
- "What did you want to say to your dad after he criticized you?"
- "Did your mom say anything after his comments? I mean, she was sitting right there!"

If you can't listen, tell her.

Sometimes you're not prepared to actively listen to your wife. You're far better off telling her that right up front than doing a poor listening job and making her feel angry, hurt, and disgusted. Maybe you're tired. Preoccupied. Stressed. Angry. Sick. Or right at the end of an exciting sporting event on television.

Say something like this: "Honey, I'm sorry, but I can't listen to you now. I'm not in the right frame of mind. I'm [whatever the reason is]. Let's schedule a time right now to talk about it, OK?" Then schedule the time, and put it on your pad and in your Day-Timer or iPhone so you don't forget. If it's going to be part of your next talk time, put it on the talk-time schedule.

Talk Back

Leading her by scheduling talk times and overseeing the use of the talk-time schedule is important. Guiding the content and flow of your talk times is important. Listening smart is important. What you say to her and how you say it is important too.

Tell a story with details.

When you're telling her about something that happened to you, force yourself to be more detailed. Don't give her just the broad, general sketch: "I had a good day." "I had a bad day." "Work was OK." "The interview went fine." "I've had better days." "Work is work." What do these comments tell her? Nothing!

She needs to know you so she can get closer to you. To meet this need, you must share the events of your day in more detail. Share what happened, where it happened, when it happened, why you think it happened, who was involved, and how you feel about what happened.

When in doubt, tell her more. This is like doing a complicated math problem. You can just give the final answer or you can show the work you did to get to the solution. Show her your work. You'll never be as detailed and descriptive as she is, but do your best.

Being logical is OK at first. That's who you are and how your mind works. After your logical—and as-detailed-as-possible—sharing, take the time to process what you've said and find your emotional, personal reaction to it. Jot the topic on your pad, put it on the talk-time schedule, and carry the topic over to the next talk time.

As you process for a day or two, let yourself go emotionally. Allow yourself to feel the raw, intense emotions connected to the event you told her about in the first conversation. Drop your brave, macho, logical front and dig up your feelings. Here's a breakdown of how that might look:

- First talk: Give the details of a confrontation with your boss at work. What happened, what people said, what they did, etc.
- Processing time: Think about the confrontation, and pray that God will help you identify and feel your emotions. Jot down on your pad what you feel.
- Second talk: "Honey, I've been processing that confrontation with my boss. He had no right to treat me that way. I'm angry and feel betrayed and used. I'm discouraged. I'm also scared, because I wonder if I'm going to lose my job. It reminds me of how my dad used to treat me, and..."

Here are some conversational topics that have a pretty good chance of leading to emotional connection and intimacy with your wife:

- An event that triggered strong emotions, whether positive (such as happiness, relief, or joy) or difficult (like anger, frustration, rage, despair, discouragement, or hurt)
- A stressful situation or interaction you experienced with someone
- Any comment or question about your marriage: "How are we doing as a couple?" "Do you feel close to me this week?" "You seem distant these past few hours/days—what's going on?" "Am I meeting your needs this week?"
- Spiritual issues, such as how you are doing in your relationship with God, what you're learning in your quiet times this week, what you're learning in your Bible study at church, or how God is guiding you lately. Ask her to comment on these same spiritual areas in her life.

Husband, as you go through your day, jot down topics like these on your pad. Think about them, and also jot down what comes to mind. At the next talk time, share what's on your pad.

It's your job to be the pursuer and leader in communicating with your wife. Most husbands never step up in this area. God wants you to be the exception. Your wife needs you to be the exception. It's not easy. I know, because it's not easy for me. But by following the strategies in this chapter, you can get it done.

Build Your Happily-Ever-After Marriage

1. Husband, do you believe you are responsible for leading your wife in the area of communication? Will you agree to lead by creating regular talk times each week and supervising the use of the talk-time schedule? What obstacles will you have to overcome to lead in this way?
2. Right now, schedule your four talk times for this week. Also, create a talk-time schedule and post it.
3. Husband, what do you think and feel about my description of a talk time? Which steps will be easier for you to do, and which ones will be harder for you?
4. Husband, tell your wife what kind of listener you think you are. Now, ask her what kind of listener she thinks you are. Which of the listening principles in this chapter are you willing to practice?
5. Husband, which of the talking principles described in this chapter are you willing to apply? Will you use a pad or electronic device to jot down or record topics to process, and will you share those topics with your wife?

6. At the end of each talk time during the next month, take a few minutes and discuss how the time went: what worked, what didn't work, and how you can improve your communication.

Chapter Seven

MISTAKE #5: WIFE, YOU'RE ALLOWING MISTREATMENT

Speak Up and Don't Be a Doormat

REMEMBER HOW CINDERELLA endured all the terrible, cruel treatment from her mean stepmother and her worthless stepsisters? She slaved away all day, doing every menial and thankless task in the house. Her performance was never good enough, and she often had to do jobs over again. Her family constantly criticized and belittled her. No one cared about her needs.

Through it all, Cinderella kept her cheerful attitude and continued serving her nasty relatives with barely a word of complaint. She always believed things would just work out someday and that the prince would carry her off to his castle.

Cinderella's story is a fairy tale, but I believe it has deeper meaning. Chances are very good that you are living out this story in your marriage. How so, you ask? This is how: You are allowing your husband to mistreat you, and you're doing nothing about it. You are today's version of Cinderella, continuing to be the best wife you can be in the face of poor treatment from your husband. You hope and pray for change, but you take no action to create that change.

The odds of your husband suddenly and miraculously treating you better are about as good as the odds of Cinderella getting the prince. I know she did get the prince, but hers is a completely fictional story. A fantasy! Unless you do something, your husband will continue to treat you with a lack of sensitivity, understanding, and love.

If you act like a doormat, you'll become a doormat.

What Is Mistreatment?

Here's my definition of *mistreatment* by a husband: any violation of biblical instruction about his role as a husband. Here are six biblical roles your husband is to fulfill:

1. To love you as Christ loved the church (Eph. 5:25)
2. To lead you in every area (Eph. 5:23–24) as a Christlike servant (Matt. 20:28; John 13:3–5)
3. To treat you softly, gently, and with tender care (1 Pet. 3:7; 1 Cor. 7:33; Col. 3:19)

4. To be a godly man (Matt. 22:36–37)
5. To energetically pursue you in romance (Song of Songs)
6. To constantly build you up with compliments and encouraging words (Prov. 31:28–29; Song of Songs)

If he fails to treat you as these verses instruct him, he is mistreating you. I know these standards are high, but they describe the way God wants your husband to act toward you.

More specifically, husbands mistreat their wives in two ways.

Verbal mistreatment includes criticism that is not constructive but offensive. It includes personal attacks on your character, behavior, or appearance. Sarcasm. Belittling, demeaning comments. Raising his voice to you in anger. Swearing. Name-calling. Mocking. Mentioning divorce.

Behavioral mistreatment includes ignoring you. Sharing his view and not listening to yours. Throwing things or doing property damage. Failing again and again to do chores. Making promises and breaking them. Making decisions without you. Lack of romance. Refusing to have sex with you. Refusing to help with the kids. Controlling behavior. Selfish behavior.

The bottom line is this: If you feel mistreated by your husband, he has almost certainly mistreated you. In other words, you define mistreatment—he doesn't. If you feel angry and hurt by something he says or does, he has mistreated you.

Here's one exception: You may have somehow misunderstood or misinterpreted something he said or did. Even in a case like this, you still need to bring up the issue and talk it through.

Even Good Husbands Mistreat

Now, in this chapter, I'm not referring to husbands who are bona fide, abusive dirt balls. This chapter is not designed to help you deal with a husband who is involved in some form of serious, out-of-control sin, such as an affair, physical violence, sexual addiction like the watching of pornography and/or movies that degrade sex and dishonor marriage, drug or alcohol addiction, gambling, refusing to work for a living, or vicious verbal attacks. If your husband is sinning in one of these areas, you'll need to mount a dramatic, aggressive, tough-love campaign involving the help of others. Get my book *I Don't Love You Anymore.*

I'm writing here about good, decent husbands who are mistreating their wives. Even when the husband is this kind of man—someone who is well-intentioned—this kind of insensitivity is still very serious and does damage to you, to him, to the kids, and to your marriage. My experience indicates that it is happening in many marriages.

Stop the Cinderella Thinking

Your insensitive husband is mistreating you, and you're doing zero about it. He's not a bad guy. In fact, he's a good guy. And he does love you. But mistreatment is still mistreatment, and his behavior is limiting your marital intimacy. And this is a serious loss!

You put up with mistreatment because you believe one of two Cinderella-thinking mistakes. First, you may believe that if you just keep on faithfully loving him and meeting his needs, he'll eventually stop hurting you and treat you with more sensitivity and love. Wrong. He doesn't even realize he's mistreating you. If you don't tell him, he'll never know. He sees you acting as though you are content. He watches you do all the usual things for him. So he figures everything in the marriage is fine. The fact that he is limiting your intimacy won't dawn on him. Remember, he's a man.

By the way, how is your "change him with love and kindness" approach working? You've been at it now for a number of years. Yeah, I thought so. Not changing, is he?

You may be wondering if my counsel agrees with 1 Peter 3:1–2: "Likewise you wives, be submissive to your own husbands, so that if any do not obey the word, they may be won without a word by the conduct of their wives, as they see the purity and reverence of your lives." These verses teach submission, not subservience or passivity. The wife is always to model purity and excellent behavior, but she is also to follow the verses that instruct her to speak up in a loving and firm way. The Proverbs 31 wife was submissive, but she was also very assertive and active, and her husband respected her. Also, other passages teach that we should confront sin (Matt. 18:15–17) and speak the truth (Eph. 4:15; Col. 3:9).

My conclusion is this: When you look at the whole of Scripture, you see God instructing wives to model submission and excellent behavior *and* to be assertive and worthy of respect. (In my book *The Top Ten Most Outrageous Couples of the Bible* I explain that submission on the wife's part never means not using her intelligence, her abilities, her ideas, or her personality in her marriage.)

Second, you may believe that your man isn't that bad and that you'll be OK if he doesn't change. You say to yourself at least a hundred times a week: "Hey, he's a good man. He works hard at his job. He goes to church. He doesn't beat me, drink like a fish, or sleep around. He could be a lot worse. I have to accept the fact that he won't change. I can live with that."

You've given up hope of ever having a deeper, more intimate bond with your husband. His insensitive words and behavior do hurt, but you think they can't be helped. You just paint on your brave smile and ride the Cinderella coach on that long, lonely road to the horizon.

Some older wives in your church family or social circle may have convinced you that the man you have is as good as he can be. They've persuaded you that men are "just that way" and that you can do nothing about it. For good measure, they may have thrown in the classic enabler line: "Honey, you just have to make Jesus your husband."

These two Cinderella ways of thinking are wrong. Wrong, wrong, wrong. If you believe your husband will change because of your excellent behavior as a wife, you're sadly mistaken. If you believe your husband can't change and you tolerate his mistreatment, you are in error. In both cases, *you* are part of the problem. You are enabling him to stay exactly the kind of husband he is now. He's convinced you're OK with who he is, so he has absolutely zero motivation to do anything differently.

Are you guilty of one of these Cinderella mistakes? It's time to get rid of your evening gown and glass slippers. Stop being so nice and forgiving and fake all the time. Start being honest with yourself and him.

The Dialogue

Wife: I'm just a nice person. I can't help but be nice to him.

Me: No, you're not nice. You aren't telling him the truth, as you are instructed to do in Ephesians 4:25, Colossians 3:9, and many other places in Scripture. That's not being nice. And you aren't giving your husband a chance to change. That's not nice, either. You're also allowing your children to learn that it's OK to mistreat a woman. That, too, is not nice. You aren't nice; you're codependent.

Wife: But I have to submit to him, don't I?

Me: No, not when he's sinning. You don't submit to sin. Rather, you confront it every time. (See Matthew 18:15–17.)

Wife: I don't get angry with my husband. It's not ladylike or Christlike.

Me: First, you *are* angry deep down. Second, it's OK and healthy to be angry. We're actually commanded to express it the same day we feel it (Eph. 4:26–27.) Third, Christ became angry, and for good reason (Matt. 21:12–13; Mark 8:32–33), and He expressed it. You have good reason to be angry too.

Wife: He always says he's sorry after doing or saying something that hurts me.

Me: Sorry isn't good enough. True repentance is what is required and may include being sorry but focuses on change. If you're OK with him just saying he's sorry, that's all he's going to give you.

Wife: Most of the time he's blunt and abrasive because he's had a hard, stressful day at work.

Me: So? That's no excuse. Sinful behavior is sinful behavior. Treating you roughly is not an acceptable or effective way to handle his stress. Speaking of stress, his behavior is causing *you* stress, isn't it?

Wife: I saw my mom take mistreatment from my dad for years. I guess that's where I learned to put up with it. To me, it is normal. My ex-husband also treated me with insensitivity too much of the time.

Me: Your mom was your codependent Yoda. She taught you to tolerate mistreatment. But you can change that pattern and stop the generational sin. We'll work in therapy on your past pain, and that will help you be more assertive with your husband.

Wife: I'm afraid to stand up to him. Will he get really angry and be out of control? Will he put up a fight and battle me? Will my changed behavior disrupt the kids' lives? Will he leave me or maybe even divorce me? Will I find out he doesn't love me enough to change?

Me: These are valid fears. When you start standing up to him, you may be in for a battle. He's used to mistreating you and getting away with it. He won't like getting static from you. You have to decide that following the Bible and finding your assertive, person-of-value, Christlike voice is best for everyone in the family. If you want to be treated well and build a close marriage, you must demand good treatment. If he's truly a good man, he will change in response to your changes.

Your Five-Step Assertiveness Program

I've led many wives through these five steps of assertiveness training. I've seen them work over and over again. Now it's your turn.

Step 1: Sign up a support person

You can't carry off this assertiveness program on your own. It's too tough. You need to find one married female Christian (not a family member) who is willing to provide frequent encouragement and accountability. She could be a close friend or mentor, such as a leader in your church or a pastor's wife.

You'll tell her everything about your husband's mistreatment and how you've tolerated it. You'll ask her to keep you on the assertiveness track by praying with you, asking you to share with her how you're being assertive, giving you pep talks when needed, calling you a wimp when you falter, and gently but firmly getting you back in the saddle.

Meet with her once a week, and stay in touch by phone. Call her when you need to vent or get some encouragement. The Bible teaches us to "bear one another's burdens" (Gal. 6:2), and that's exactly what your support person is going to do.

Step 2: Keep a mistreatment journal

Buy a small pad and record every instance of your husband's mistreatment. You can also do this on your phone or computer. Use three columns: one for what happened, one for your emotional reaction, and one for what you did about it. Do this for two weeks, and you'll get a pretty good baseline measurement of the mistreatment episodes. You may be surprised at how many or how few instances you record.

Your journal will help you track the frequency of mistreatment and the specific nature of it. When does it usually happen? Does it follow a recognizable pattern? What forms does it take? How long does it last? What exact words and behaviors does he exhibit?

The journal will also help you understand the mistreatment and your reaction to it. What emotions do you have when it happens? What fearful thoughts come into your mind? What do you usually do in response?

Initially of course, you will not be jotting down any impressive, assertive responses. You'll jot down your usual, wimpy responses. As you improve, you'll be able to write more healthy, assertive behaviors. This will motivate and encourage you.

Share your journal with your support person. Going over it with her (and your therapist, if you have one) will greatly enhance the learning process. If your husband wants to know what you're using the journal for, tell him. It's no secret. Tell him it's a tool to help you be more honest and assertive with him when he mistreats you. If he's willing and has a good attitude, the two of you can go over the journal together. It can also help *him* correct his insensitive behavior.

Step 3: Keep to one-way communication every time

Using the one-way communication technique I explained in chapter 5, tell him *every time* he mistreats you. That's right, every time. A breach of respect has occurred and caused some damage, and your job is to let him know as soon as possible. Tell him the truth in a loving way (Eph. 4:15). Be brief. Just a few sentences will get the job done.

If you can't verbally point out his mistake immediately, at least do it by the end of the day. As Ephesians 4:26–27 commands, you need to clean out difficult, painful emotions each day. You could use part of a regularly scheduled talk time to lay it on him.

Tell him your emotions and what he did, and ask him (when he's ready) to apologize and talk the situation out. Then walk away or be silent. What you say could go like this:

> Honey, I have something difficult to say to you. I was angry and hurt by your sarcastic comment this morning about my cooking ability. I felt insulted. When you're ready, I'd like to hear an apology and discuss what happened.

If you stuff your emotions and say nothing, a lot of bad things happen. You may stuff and stuff and then periodically blow up in anger. You may get depressed. You may become bitter and resentful. His behavior will never change. Worst of all, you run the risk of hitting the wall one day and leaving the marriage because all your love is gone.

Step 4: Tell him why you think he mistreated you

Your man has zero insight into why he mistreats you. He probably doesn't even realize he's doing it at all. Pointing out his mistreatment in the one-way manner is good, but it's not enough. On his own, he still won't try to figure out why he acts in insensitive, hurtful ways. Seeking an explanation for his poor relationship skills would mean digging into personal matters, and he's spent his whole life staying away from those sensitive areas.

Your job is to use well-placed, one-way observations to show him the reasons you think he mistreats you. He has a relationship disability. An integral part of the rehabilitation process is having a coach who will show him exactly where it comes from. You are that coach. He's not asking for your help, but you're going to give it to him anyway. The insights you share can play a big part in his change process. You won't give him this kind of insight every time because you won't always have an opinion about the reason. But when you do have a good guess, tell him. For example:

> That temper outburst last night reminded me of your dad. You look and act just like him when you lose it. Until you deal with him and your feelings about how he raised you, you'll keep on raging and hurting me and the kids.
>
> When I said no to sex this morning, you shut me out and ignored me for three hours. You still haven't healed from your ex-wife rejecting you sexually and in other ways. So when you feel like I've rejected you, you close down and won't talk about it. When you're ready, I want you to talk to me about what she did to you. When that pain is out of you, you'll be able to open up to me and receive all my love.
>
> You're stuffing your work stress again tonight. You've got the television on, and you've been avoiding me for the past two hours. I'm hurt and frustrated. If you'd share the work problems with me, you'd be happier, and we'd be closer. But that's up to you.
>
> The past month, you've pulled back from me. You're preoccupied with your work and sports. You don't seem too happy with me or your life. I think one of the reasons is that you've drifted

> from the Lord. You're not having regular quiet times, and you have not gone to church with us three Sundays in a row. I'm hurt that you're shutting me out, and I'm also concerned about you. If you want to talk about what's going on and want my help to get back on track spiritually, find me, and we'll talk.
>
> Did you notice what you just did? Our conversation was starting to get a little personal, so you made a joke to lighten the mood. That's something you do a lot. It ticks me off because I need closeness with you. I've seen your dad and brother do the same joke thing to avoid personal subjects. I'd like to talk about this and what we can do about it. When you're ready, let me know, and we'll schedule a time to talk.

Step 5: Give him a consequence

Most often, individuals change only when they experience sufficient pain to motivate new behavior. Being honest and direct with him is important, but it won't be enough to motivate him to work on changing his insensitive ways. He must face some consequences for his mistreatment of you or he won't feel the need to change.

Use the one-way technique, and tell him you'll wait for his heartfelt apology and willingness to discuss the incident fully. You want to see him try to figure out why he mistreated you. During this waiting period, before he comes back to you, the marriage is temporarily suspended. You're still married, but not in the same "everything's OK and normal" way. If everything seems fine, he has no reason to apologize and work at resolving the issue.

So everything must *not* be fine. You will be quiet, reserved, and pulled back from him. There's to be no real communication about any other topic, no affection, and no time together until he returns and is genuinely involved in talking about what happened.

No sex, either, until he's truly repentant. *Repentant* means being sorry, listening and reflecting back as you vent, and working to uncover why he mistreated you. I have a funny feeling the temporary suspension of sex may get his attention. You sometimes need to suspend marital sex (1 Cor. 7:5), and this is one of those times. To engage in the intensely vulnerable and intimate act of intercourse before resolving a breach of respect (or at least before the process is begun) is very harmful to you, and you need to tell him that. The male way of resolving the problem is having sex. That's not your way, and it won't work for you.

It may take you a while to learn these assertiveness steps. Confronting his mistreatment won't be easy, but the benefits will be worth the effort. You will clean your system of anger and hurt and resentment. You will be able to forgive. You will stay emotionally healthy. You will give him repeated opportunities and motivation to change. You'll stay in love with him. And together you can build a more intimate bond.

Build Your Happily-Ever-After Marriage

1. Ask your husband to tell you if he sees ways he mistreats you. Ask him why he thinks he acts in those ways.
2. Being gentle but honest, tell your husband how he mistreats you—what he says and what he does. If you have any ideas as to why he makes these mistakes, share them with him.
3. Which of the two Cinderella mistakes are you guilty of making? To which of the reasons or excuses in the Dialogue section can you relate? What are you afraid might happen if you speak up and show assertiveness with your husband?
4. Which of the five assertiveness steps are you willing to try at this time? Which one would be the most effective for you?
5. Ask your husband what consequences would motivate him to change his mistreatment of you.
6. Discuss how he can avoid consequences.

Chapter Eight

MISTAKE #6: HUSBAND, YOU'RE BEING INSENSITIVE

Be Gentle and Earn Her Respect

MALE INSENSITIVITY BEGAN back in the Garden of Eden, when Adam blamed Eve for the first sin. When God asked him if he had eaten from the forbidden tree, Adam responded, "The woman whom You gave to be with me, she gave me fruit of the tree, and I ate" (Gen. 3:12).

Talk about your lame excuses! What a weasel! Instead of protecting his wife, he tried to pin the sin on her. Eve must have been thinking, "Thanks a lot, Adam. Your support makes me feel so special."

Adam was the first insensitive man, but he certainly wasn't the last. A man, by nature, has an insensitive streak a mile wide. He tends to be selfish, crude, dense, rough around the conversational edges, controlling, sarcastic, flippant, blunt, forgetful, and devoid of any ability to understand a woman.

Hey! I have a great idea! Let's put this incredibly insensitive man into a relationship with an unbelievably sensitive woman. Yeah, and let's have them get married and live together. What could go wrong?

Actually just about everything.

Do you think the woman, with her built-in hair-trigger sensitivity, will get angry and hurt by her bull-in-the-china-shop man? You'd better believe it. This dramatic difference in sensitivity is a major challenge in marriage.

It Doesn't Take Much

It doesn't take much to upset your woman. She's emotional, moody, and easily offended. She watches you like a hawk and misses nothing. She scrutinizes everything you say and do and runs it through her sensitivity grid. Something you consider trivial and inconsequential is very likely to feel like a personal attack to her. A word, a glance, a sigh, or a certain tone of voice can cause an intense reaction of pain in her. She may not tell you, but inside she's hurt and feeling unloved and mistreated.

Here's one small example of how difficult dealing with a sensitive wife can be. Out of nowhere, she says to you, "I'm getting fat." That comment is shocking enough, but she's also looking at you intently and expecting a response. This is a classic no-win situation for you, the hapless man. Regardless of what you say, you will be insensitive and wrong and offensive.

You could say, "No, you're not fat." Then she would say, "I *am* fat! I just told you I was fat. I think I know what fat is. Check out these thighs. Would you call them thin?"

Or you could say nothing. That won't work either. She'll say, "Didn't you hear me? I said I was fat. What we have here is a fat wife who is being ignored by her husband. I know you think I'm overweight and unattractive. That's why you're not saying anything."

You could say, "Well, honey, I guess you have gained a few pounds. So have I. No big deal." Now you're dead meat, even though you have told the truth. "I knew it!" she says. "I knew you thought I was fat. How long have you thought I was fat?" Good luck answering that last question without offending her.

Treat Her Like a Queen

The "I'm getting fat" scenario is just one tiny example of the challenge you face in living with a hypersensitive woman. Learning to be sensitive and understanding is difficult, but you can do it. Scripture makes it clear that you must treat her like a queen.

Jesus loved women and treated them with dignity and respect. To Him, they were equal in value to men. This was revolutionary thinking for His culture. Jesus shocked the Jewish world by being the first rabbi to allow women to be His disciples. He invited Mary, Martha, and Mary

Magdalene (who might have been a former prostitute) into His inner circle. Jesus is our example, men.

The key verse about how to treat a wife is 1 Peter 3:7. Read this verse very carefully, husband, because it packs quite a punch:

> Likewise, you husbands, live considerately with your wives, giving honor to the woman as the weaker vessel, since they too are also heirs of the grace of life, so that your prayers will not be hindered.

God commands you to treat your wife as a precious, priceless person. You are to treat her better than anyone else on earth. She is your equal and deserves your expression of dignity and respect. You are to handle her gently, kindly, and softly. You are to adore and cherish her. You are to express the utmost tenderness toward her.

If you fail to treat her with this kind of understanding and sensitivity, your selfishness will block your access to God—the passage says that if you treat her right, "your prayers will not be hindered." If you treat her wrong, your most urgent and heartfelt requests of God may go unanswered. That's the worst possible consequence and shows how important this is to God. Treat her well, or your spiritual life will suffer. One of the main reasons so many husbands are spiritually dry is that they mistreat their wives—whether they mean to or not.

The Checklist of Sensitivity

I've compiled a list of many common insensitive husband behaviors. It's not exhaustive, by any means, but it will help you get a good idea of how insensitive you are and where you need to improve. Check the ones you feel apply to you. If you're not sure, ask your wife. She'll know.

Verbal mistreatment

Mr. Logic

- ✓ "You don't know what you're talking about."
- ✓ "You're not making any sense."
- ✓ "You're too emotional."
- ✓ "Here's what I'd do in the situation if I were you."
- ✓ "That's life, honey."
- ✓ "Let it go. It's in the past."
- ✓ Interrupting her and telling her she's wrong to feel or think a certain way
- ✓ Telling her how to feel or think
- ✓ Playing devil's advocate and defending the person who has hurt or angered her

The Wonderful World of Sarcasm

- ✓ "Oh, you're perfect, I guess."

- ✓ "It has to be your way, doesn't it?"
- ✓ "Who died and made you queen?"
- ✓ "Oh, sure, that'll work."

Avoiding Intimate Conversations

- ✓ Refusing to talk
- ✓ Ignoring her when she's talking about something you don't want to talk about
- ✓ Being cynical
- ✓ Cracking a joke to lighten the mood and prevent the conversation from getting too deep

Poor Conflict-Resolution Skills

- ✓ Raising your voice
- ✓ Refusing to listen to her side of the argument
- ✓ Leaving and not coming back to restart the conversation
- ✓ Making personal attacks
- ✓ Laughing at her feelings and opinions
- ✓ Lying to her to avoid conflict

Criticism

- ✓ Throwing barbs about her cooking, her housecleaning, her parenting, her spending, her weight or appearance, her family, or her intelligence

Behavioral mistreatment

✓ Controlling the remote

✓ Being lazy and not doing your share of the chores

✓ Forgetting to do chores

✓ Promising and not delivering

✓ Forgetting special days like her birthday, your anniversary, Valentine's Day, and Mother's Day

✓ Remembering special days but not doing much for her

✓ Doing your own fun activities and leaving her with the kids

✓ Working too many hours and not telling her when you'll be home

✓ Refusing to do activities she enjoys doing

✓ Controlling the money

✓ Giving her a monthly allowance

✓ Making financial decisions without consulting her

✓ Driving like a maniac

✓ Refusing to spend time with her relatives

✓ Pressuring her or forcing her to have sex without the proper emotional and spiritual preparation

✓ Not changing the toilet paper roll

✓ Not lifting or lowering the toilet seat

✓ Not cleaning your whiskers from the sink after you shave

✓ Belching and not saying "Excuse me"

Do any of these verbal or behavioral examples of mistreatment look familiar? I certainly could check off quite a few. Be man enough to admit your mistakes and work on correcting them.

The Dialogue

Husband: I don't mean to hurt her with what I say and do.

Me: You are hurting her whether you mean to or not.

Husband: She's too sensitive.

Me: No, she's a woman. They're all sensitive. You are too insensitive.

Husband: I can't listen to her when she's venting about something I've said or done wrong. She takes way too long.

Me: She needs to vent, and she'll talk about what happened until she knows you understand. Listen, reflect, and have a good attitude, and you can shorten the time of suffering. If you resist, you'd better get comfortable.

Husband: I don't want to become some overly sensitive wimp of a man. I'm a man's man.

Me: A real man learns to be sensitive to his wife. Jesus was the ultimate Man, and He was sensitive to women. Of course, you can stay a macho man and have a miserable wife and a mediocre marriage. It's up to you.

Husband: I can't be perfect!

Me: Nobody's asking you to be perfect. With God's help and your hard work, you will improve dramatically. She can live with a certain amount of insensitivity as long as you're being sensitive most of the time.

Your Five-Step Sensitivity Program

In the previous chapter, I took your dear wife through five steps of assertiveness training. Now it's time for you to learn how to be sensitive.

Step 1: Sign up a support person

Just as your wife needs someone to come alongside her in her assertiveness program, you also need a support person. Don't play Lone Ranger. You'll never make it. Read the Support Person section in chapter 7 and follow those same guidelines. Find a trustworthy, married, Christian man. Tell him all about your insensitivity. Ask him to hold you accountable in your sensitivity efforts and failures, pray with him, meet with him once a week, and stay in touch by phone. If he's open to it, you may hold him accountable in his areas of insensitivity toward his wife too.

Step 2: Keep a mistreatment journal

Read the mistreatment journal section of chapter 7, and follow the steps I outline there. Buy a pad and make a note every time you mistreat your wife. Use three columns: one for what you did or said, one for your emotional reaction, and one for what you did after the incident (such as walked away, apologized, or acted as though it never happened).

Keep the journal for two weeks. You'll learn how often you mistreat your wife and exactly how you do it. You may be able to identify what factors trigger you to act in these insensitive ways, such as stress, fatigue, feeling controlled, wanting to maintain control, or spiritual apathy. Your wife will be keeping her journal at the same time. Every few days or at least once a week, sit down with her to compare journals. Finding out how each of you views the episodes of mistreatment will be interesting and instructive.

Step 3: Urge her to catch you

Give your wife permission to catch you every time you are being insensitive. This is good for her assertiveness and good for your recognition of the problem. You don't even realize you're being insensitive, so you need her to point it out. Eventually, you'll be able to catch yourself and to eliminate many of the insensitive episodes.

Provide her with a code phrase (women love codes, remember?) to use to alert you to your insensitivity, such as "I think you're being insensitive," "I believe you've crossed the line," "Time out," or, "You just cost yourself sex tonight, buddy." (Just kidding about that last one.)

When you hear the code phrase, don't fight it or resist in any way. Believe your wife because she is the only one who is able to say when you're being insensitive. If she says you are, you are. Period. As soon as you hear the code phrase, do four things: Take a quick break to simmer down and chill out (saying a brief prayer would be a good idea), come back to her and apologize, pursue her if she's pulled away, and talk the situation out.

Step 4: Say you're sorry, pursue her, and talk it out

Your run-of-the-mill man doesn't apologize well. He hates to show weakness and to admit that he's wrong. Believe me, if your woman is upset, chances are very good that you've done something wrong.

First, here's how not to apologize. Don't say, "I'm sorry if I offended, hurt, or angered you." What do you mean, *if?* There's no if about it. Something you did or said actually happened, and it bothered her. Don't say, "I'm sorry, but..." The *but* cancels out the *sorry* part, and she doesn't want to hear your lame excuse. Don't say, "You misunderstood me." Now you're blaming her rather than accepting responsibility. Don't say, "we," as in, "We both got angry in that situation." *We* indicates that she is at fault too. That won't make her happy.

Don't say, "I'm sorry" in a resentful or exasperated way. If you can't say it in a heartfelt way, wait until you can. But do say you're sorry. Acting as though nothing happened further insults and hurts your wife. If you said "I'm sorry" in the wrong way, you caused additional hurt, and now you must say another "I'm sorry" for your poor apology and still repeat your "I'm sorry" in the right way for your original insensitive remark.

An effective apology includes three critical steps. First, say the initial "I'm sorry" in a heartfelt and genuine way right to her face. Use words like these: "Honey, I'm sorry. I blew it. I was wrong, and I upset you. Please forgive me. Let's talk it out when you're ready."

Second, if she gets emotional and goes silent or walks away, you must go after her. She wants you to pursue her. She wants and needs you to come to her, talk out the incident, reassure her of your love, and win her back. If she's not ready to talk, leave for a few minutes, and then come back. Keep coming back until she's ready to talk about what happened.

Third, be prepared for several talks with her about the insensitive mistake you made. She'll do all the talking and venting initially. Listen, reflect back to her what you're hearing, and continue to say, "I'm sorry." One "I'm sorry," even if sincere, is never enough for a woman. Keep saying it until she believes it.

When she has finished venting, she needs to hear from you. Without making any excuses, tell her why you think you acted in such an insensitive way. Do your best to figure out what triggered your words or behavior. If you can't think of any explanation at the time, jot down the incident on your pad and tell her you'll think on it and get back to her.

Step 5: Watch your mouth

As a man—especially an angry or frustrated man—you have a bad habit of being too harsh and abrasive when you speak to your woman. This kind of insensitivity crushes her and does real damage to her self-esteem and her respect for you.

Remember three verses when you speak to your wife. The first verse, 1 Peter 3:7, instructs husbands to be gentle. The second verse, Proverbs 16:24, tells us that pleasant words are sweet and healing. And the third verse, 1 Corinthians 13:5, simply and powerfully states that love does not act unbecomingly.

Keep your tone within reasonable limits. Avoid sarcasm and yelling. Don't use vulgar (or worse) language of any kind. Stay away from the words *never*, *always*, and *should*. Refrain from any critical personal attacks. Don't roll your eyes. Don't sigh loudly.

Communication is a self-correcting process. If you make a mistake as you're speaking—whether she catches you or you catch yourself—stop the conversation immediately and take a break. Come back, apologize for your mistake, and continue the conversation. I'll go into much more detail about the ins and outs of conflict resolution in a later chapter.

Build Your Happily-Ever-After Marriage

1. Husband, how did your dad treat your mom? Did he model insensitive behavior in his treatment of your mom? What form did this take? How did your mom react to his insensitivity?
2. Using the checklist of insensitive behaviors in this chapter, tell your wife the specific insensitive remarks and behaviors you are guilty of the most. Man up and ask her to tell you the most common ways you are insensitive to her.
3. Who can you ask to be your support person?
4. Are you willing to take the five steps in the sensitivity program? Which of the steps will be the most difficult for you? Ask your wife which of the steps are most important to her.
5. How are you in the apology department? Which of the "I'm sorry" mistakes do you make most often?

Chapter Nine

MISTAKE #7: WIFE, YOU'RE NOT BEING SEXY

Be Interested, Be Aggressive, and Be Responsive

MA'AM, YOU'D BETTER sit down and get a firm grip on the armrest. I'm going to take you where very few women have gone: into the strange, twisted, and wonderful world of your husband's sexuality. It won't be pretty, but it will be the truth. Here we go.

THE HUSBAND'S PRIORITIES

Your husband loves sex. He thinks about it constantly. You could say he's obsessed with it. In fact, go ahead and say that, because it's true. Sex is his number-one human need in life.

When women list their priorities from most important to least important, here are the typical results:

1. Children
2. Family
3. Friends
4. Home
5. Church
6. Health
7. Job
8. Finances
9. Sex

As you can see, sex is well down the list. It barely makes the list.

When men rank their priorities, here's what they come up with:

1. Sex
2. Sex
3. Sex
4. Sex
5. Sex
6. Sex
7. Sex
8. Sex
9. Food

Believe me, I'm not kidding. Ask your husband if you doubt me.

Sex and memory

As a woman, you have a phenomenal memory. You can remember what you were wearing at your third-grade piano recital. Your husband can't remember what he had for lunch today. But the one glaring exception in your incredible memory bank is your recall of sexual activity. Your husband, however, can remember everything about your sexual life as a couple.

You are consistently incorrect when you try to remember the last time you had sex with him. You almost always think it was "just a few days ago." You are wrong. Your husband can remember the exact date and time of day and what you were wearing.

You also seem to conveniently forget planned sexual encounters. During a talk the two of you had on Monday evening, he asked for sex on Wednesday evening. You will remember everything he said except the plan for sex. He will forget everything you said but the plan for sex.

Give that man an award!

You think your husband is always chasing you for sex. Well, he is. For him, three or four days without sex seem like an eternity. In wife time, it's just three or four days. In husband time, it's like two or three years.

But let me tell you something that will surprise you. You have no idea how many times your husband does not pursue you for sex when he wants to. You're tired, the kids are around, it's too late, or you're busy with a project. And so your courageous man bites the bullet and forces his sexual urges to the side.

He walks down the hallway, a lonely and terribly frustrated man. He deserves an award, some kind of plaque suitable for framing for all the times he graciously forgoes sex.

Your husband needs sex.

OK, forget the award idea. But understanding your husband's God-given need for sex is very important.

Sex is like air to him. It's a big part of what makes him a man.

When he has sex with you regularly, he's confident. He feels loved by you. He feels close to you. He's at peace. He's happy. He feels like a man.

When he doesn't have sex with you regularly, just the opposite is true. He loses confidence. He feels rejected by you. He's irritable, edgy, moody, and unhappy. He feels angry and frustrated. He feels like less of a man.

I've used a lot of humor to make this point, but it's a very serious point, and you must understand and accept this: Your husband has a deep, vital need for regular sex with you.

THE BIBLE AND SEX

God makes it clear that sex is to be a healthy, regular part of a marriage relationship:

> The wife does not have authority over her own body, but the husband does. Likewise, the husband does not have authority over his own body, but the wife does. Do not deprive one another except with consent for a time, that you may give yourselves to fasting and prayer. Then come together again, so that Satan does not tempt you for lack of self-control.
>
> —1 CORINTHIANS 7:4–5

Regular intercourse is not optional. It is essential to the ongoing development of intimacy in a marriage. If you deprive, defraud, or rob each other of regular sexual activity, Satan will take full advantage and bad things will happen.

Intercourse is what gives you the "one flesh" experience (Gen. 2:24). When the two of you come together in intercourse, you are truly and completely one—spiritually, emotionally, and physically.

Wife, read the Song of Songs and carefully study the Shulammite woman. She is a great example of what every man longs for in his woman. She was a shameless flirt with Solomon. She was unashamedly sensuous. She was thrilled with Solomon's body and complimented him on his various physical parts (Songs 5:10–16). She was somewhat self-conscious about her appearance (Song 1:6), but that didn't stop her from desiring Solomon and asking him to pursue her sexually (Songs 1:2–4; 3:1–4; 7:10–13).

The clear message in all these passages from the Bible, especially in the Song of Songs, is that both the husband and the wife are to enjoy sex. Sex is not a service you perform for him. It is a deeper, more intense need for him, but God also made you to need it.

For you, as for many wives, sex may be a difficult part of marriage. You will probably have to learn to experience sex as God designed it to be: pleasurable, fun, playful, stress-reducing, a wonderful escape, and a deep expression of love and intimacy. Men, though they certainly can have sexual hang-ups, usually are more naturally inclined to experience sex in those ways.

Let's look at some of the obstacles preventing you from letting yourself go and enjoying God's gift of sex with your husband.

THE DIALOGUE

WIFE: I'm not that interested in sex because he doesn't prepare me for it. We don't talk that much, we don't pray together, and he's not known for his romance. I need to be emotionally and spiritually connected to him before I can give myself to him physically. And I need more help with the chores so I'm not exhausted by the end of the day.

ME: You know what? You've hit the nail on the head. These are all valid reasons for you not to be that into sex. You need to sit him down and gently but firmly lay these concerns on him. If he wants an energetic and responsive woman in bed, he needs to improve in these areas of preparation. Applying these principles will certainly make a big difference.

WIFE: I think I just go through the motions sexually because of all my resentments against him. He's a good guy, but over the years he has hurt and disappointed me many times. I've held in my anger, and that's keeping me from opening up to him sexually. I give him sex, but it's like a duty.

ME: Sit him down, and tell him what you just told me. Take a week and write him a letter describing all the times he hurt you in the past. Ask God to help you remember all the resentments you need to include. The purpose of this letter is to release your pain in an honest, non-attacking, direct way and to forgive him. Pray that God will use the letter to bring about forgiveness. Then sit down with him, and read the letter to him. Ask your husband to listen, then reflect back to you what he hears you saying. Ask him to try to feel your pain. Take several weeks and have a number of talks in which you verbally vent about the letter's contents. If he can reflect and understand, healing and forgiveness will happen.

Wife: I have personal baggage from my past that stops me from enjoying sex.

Me: Past personal pain often causes sexual blocks. Guilt over premarital sex, abuse received as a child, rape, an abortion, a poor relationship with dad, unresolved issues with an ex-spouse, and other painful experiences need to be faced so healing can occur. Tell your husband what your past pain is, and go with him to a Christian professional therapist to work it through. Do it together.

Wife: The truth is, my husband is the one who resists sex. I want sex but I have to chase him and pressure him to get it.

Me: About 25 percent of husbands fall into this category. If you're doing all you can to be sexy and show interest and he's not responding, then he's the one with the sexual problem. (Though, of course, you must consider it "our" problem.) It could have many causes, including unresolved past pain, resentments against you, too much stress, his age, fatigue, or lack of confidence in his ability to perform. Sit him down and share your concerns. Ask him to tell you—when he's ready—what is blocking him. Use one-way communication to express your feelings each time he resists you sexually. If he won't talk it through with you, urge him to go to a Christian therapist with you. If he refuses to work on this problem, continue one-way communication as needed, and pull back from him emotionally and physically. Seeing that he's losing you may motivate him to get help.

How to Prepare for Great Sex

Great sex is all about preparation. No couple can just spontaneously jump into bed and engage in passionate, meaningful, "one flesh" sex. Here are six progressive steps that will prepare you and your husband for healthy sex.

Step 1: Schedule sex

Every weekend, on a Saturday or Sunday, sit down with your husband and schedule your sexual times for the upcoming week. This kind of planning has many benefits:

- You'll make sure sex happens even when life is busy.
- Your husband won't be in excruciating limbo, wondering when he can have sex.
- He won't need to pressure you.
- You won't have to put up with his usual crude and rather clumsy way of asking for sex.

- Both of you will be able to prepare for these special sexual periods.

Step 2: Release your stress

When a man is stressed, he sees sex as a way to escape it and release it. When a woman is stressed, she sees sex as just one more stressful event. As a wife, you must find healthy ways to vent and release your stress before you'll be ready for sex.

Talk out your daily stress with friends. Talk it out with God in prayer. Talk it out with your husband. Try releasing your stress by writing it in a journal. Read the Bible and meditate on God's Word to relieve stress. Try some basic relaxation exercises, such as tensing and relaxing your muscles from your toes to your head.

Step 3: Exercise regularly

If you expect to keep your physical intimacy intact, you (and your husband) have to stay in shape. We peak physically at eighteen years of age. After that, it's a long slide down the cliff. Unless you establish a regular program of exercise, you'll end up a flabby, pitiful couch potato. You are undoubtedly over eighteen, so let's get to work.

You need to exercise to be as attractive as possible to your mate. Do the best with the body you have. Also, exercise is the only way to fight fatigue. I see so many couples in their twenties, thirties, and forties—young couples in their prime years—who tell me, "Oh, Dr. Clarke, we'd like to have sex, but we're just too tired at the end of the day." I reply, "Really? Too tired, are we?

What kind of regular exercise program does each of you follow?" I'm usually met with complete silence.

You must have energy to be physically intimate and to be emotionally intimate. Talking takes energy too. If I didn't exercise, I couldn't possibly listen to Sandy and be a good conversationalist. You think I like riding the stationary bike three days a week for twenty minutes at a crack? I hate it! I hate that bike! I say nasty things to it when I pass by it in the mornings. I like getting off that bike. Then I go looking for Sandy. She's usually hiding somewhere in the house. It's a little game we play.

Step 4: Employ teamwork on chores

Tell your husband that if he wants a responsive sexual partner, he needs to hold up his end of the household chores and the kid jobs. If he fails to come through, he'll be making love to someone who's asleep or at least exhausted and resentful.

Step 5: Prioritize touching, talking, and praying

These three areas are essential in preparing for intercourse. You can do them during your talk times four days a week and at other, more spontaneous times.

First, you need to have plenty of non-intercourse touching throughout the week, such as kissing, making out, fondling, and massaging. Many couples touch in significant ways only as part of foreplay. That's not enough touching. Touching without intercourse (outside of sexual relations) will keep you connected and physically close between the times of intercourse.

Talking and praying together during your talk times will give you the emotional and spiritual connection you need to engage in successful intercourse. On the day you have planned to have sex, make sure you talk and pray first. You'll be amazed at the difference this will make.

Step 6: Be more aggressive sexually

Your husband opens the door to your home, and you're standing there wearing nothing but a skimpy negligee and a smile. You give him a big, wet kiss and say with a throaty, low voice, "My man is home, and I know what he needs. I need the same thing. Bad. The kids are at a neighbor's house for a few hours. I thought we could...I don't know...play a card game or do the bills together. Ha! I'm kidding! I want your body. I've been waiting all day, and I can't wait any longer. I think you know the way to the bedroom, big boy. Stud. Take me, I'm yours."

This might be a little over the top, but I think you get the idea. You don't have to be some kind of vamp, but please be more aggressive sexually. Show interest in him and his body. Pursue him sexually more of the time. Get your clothes off when you're having sex. Don't cover up! He thinks your body is beautiful, so let him see it.

Read in the Song of Songs how the Shulammite woman came on to Solomon. She was one sexually aggressive lady. She actually pursued him sexually more than he pursued her. And she is your example. That's why her story is in the Bible.

Build Your Happily-Ever-After Marriage

1. Ask your husband how often he thinks about having sex with you. Ask him what sex means to him as a man and as your husband.
2. Tell your husband how strong your sexual drive is. How often do you want to have sex with him? (All couples must come to a mutually satisfying compromise regarding frequency and not leave this in limbo; one will accept fewer times than desired, and one will accept more times than desired.)
3. Tell him what is blocking you from desiring sex with him and from being a responsive partner. Is it lack of preparation, stuffed resentments, trauma, or other personal baggage? Talk about what you can do together to work through your obstacles.
4. If your husband is the one resisting sex, ask him to tell you why. Decide how you will work through his obstacles together.
5. What do you think of the six steps of preparation for sex? Which ones are you willing to apply this week?

Chapter Ten

MISTAKE #8: HUSBAND, YOU'RE NOT BEING ROMANTIC

Be a Modern-Day Solomon

HUSBAND, YOU ARE focused on sex and think about it all the time. I believe I made that point quite nicely in the previous chapter. You are unusually kind, sweet, and loving in bed during the sexual experience. Unfortunately your wife just goes through the motions and can't be sexually responsive. Have you noticed that? Do you wonder why she is less than thrilled with your sex life?

I'll tell you why. It's because you're as romantic as an old tennis shoe. Your wife has a deep longing and need for romance. The *New Oxford American Dictionary* defines *romance* as "a feeling of excitement and mystery associated with love." If she doesn't get romanced on a daily basis, she shuts down inside. She doesn't feel loved by you. She doesn't feel close to you. She literally cannot be an aroused, energetic lover.

Before and After the Wedding

Remember your dating days? Remember how sexy and passionate she was back then? Touching you. Kissing you. Making out with you. She couldn't keep her hands off you. Why was that? Because you were *romancing* her! Courting her! Charming her! Pursuing her! She responded to all your romantic words and actions with some serious emotional and physical love.

You got married and expected her vibrant, passionate love to continue. But it dried up all too quickly. Why? Because, like millions of men before you, you stopped the romance. You stopped pursuing her romantically. So she stopped responding.

Read these classic male after-the-wedding, non-romantic behaviors and see if you recognize yourself.

Hey, I have an erection!

The sum total of your romantic pursuit of your wife is getting an erection. When you notice your erection, you're ready for sex, and you think she should be too. Your erection is her signal that this is her lucky night.

Wouldn't it be great if your wife reacted by coming up real close to you and saying, "Hey, I couldn't help but notice your erection, so meet me in the bedroom in ten minutes."

Alas, that is not how it works. When she becomes aware of your arousal, she thinks, "Oh, no, not again! I'm not ready for sex." She needs more preparation than your erect male sex organ. It's enough for you but not for her.

I'm a master of asking for sex.

You have a very smooth, suave, and romantic way of asking your wife to come with you to the boudoir: "How about tonight?" "Do you think maybe...uh, you know, you and me?" "Hey, baby, got something for you." "Let's have sex tonight." (That certainly cuts to the chase.) "Is your period over?" (Obviously, you're not really concerned about her physical well-being.) "Uhh, uhh, uhh." (You grunt like a male gorilla.)

Sometimes you don't even make a sound. You come up behind her in the kitchen and grab her in that one certain way. In bed, you roll over and place your hand on her stomach. Or you snuggle up next to her and start fondling her.

Again, without any romantic buildup these crude approaches are not well received. You sense resistance, don't you? Without any warning and without any expression of romantic love, she has no choice but to flinch and be apathetic at best: "Well, OK, if you have to have it." Is that the kind of reaction you want to keep getting?

Just the television, my wife, and me

You come home in the evening after work, tired and stressed. You're glad to be home, and you just want to relax and unwind. After a nice dinner, you settle in to watch television. It helps you escape from life. You like to have your wife watch with you. You love her, of course, and want to spend time with her.

This is sad, but you consider this mutual television watching to be quality time. It gives you a warm, comfortable feeling. You feel close to your wife, and you're pretty sure she feels close to you. Ah, the good life.

The truth is, the two of you are close only in a geographical sense. Watching television together doesn't create the kind of romantic, intimate experience she longs to have with you. It works for you but not for her.

Your Woman Needs Romance

If you don't regularly romance your wife, she'll feel fat, unattractive (even ugly), uninteresting, unhappy, and unloved. That's the brutal truth. If you don't believe me, ask her. She'll probably stay married to you, and I hope she does, but your marriage will be dry as dust.

Romance is the oil that keeps a love relationship running smoothly. What happens if you drain all the oil out of your car and try to drive it? The engine will seize up and die. Your lack of romance has caused your love relationship to seize up and begin to die.

Well, that's the bad news. You stopped the romance, and your wife is cold, distant, not into sex, not warm or loving, irritable, and not too impressed with you. If things stay this way, it's going to be a long, hard trek to your golden anniversary.

The good news is that you can learn to be romantic again (or for the first time in your life) and bring back the love and passion into your woman and your marriage. The intensity and depth you experience will be better than you had back in your infatuation-fueled dating days.

Let me introduce you to two men who can help you in the romance department.

The Original Mr. Romance

The first man is Solomon. He was perhaps the greatest lover who ever lived. The story of his love life with his sweetheart and eventual wife, the Shulammite woman (whose name is not given), fills the Song of Songs.

God had Solomon write this beautiful love poem so that a caveman like you might get some critically important romantic clues. These guidelines worked thousands of years ago for Solomon, and they will work for you today.

Solomon was romantic during his courtship and throughout his entire marriage. He never stopped the romantic behaviors. He pursued his beautiful girl and expressed romantic love for her in a variety of ways. I urge you to read the whole book with your beloved, but here are just a few snapshots from Solomon's romantic repertoire:

- *Kissing her.* Some fantastic kissing happens in this book. They don't waste any time getting to each other's lips, either. The second verse in the book is a kissing verse. And get this, husband: Song of Songs 4:11

gives the clearest description you'll ever read of French kissing!

- *Touching and making out with her.* Solomon and the Shulammite were real make-out artists. You'll find some very erotic touching and fondling going on in Song of Songs 2:6; 8:3. PG-13, baby!
- *Complimenting her.* Solomon compliments his woman throughout the book. He can't say enough nice things about her. He describes her body in loving detail (Songs 4:1–7; 7:1–9). I mean, *whoa!* He calls the Shulammite the "most beautiful among women" (Songs 1:8). What woman wouldn't just love to hear that—*often*—from her man?
- *Listening to her.* Solomon clearly mastered the skill of listening to his woman. He hangs on her every word. He even tells her he loves the sound of her voice (Songs 2:14).

How did the Shulammite respond to Solomon's romantic pursuit of her? With an undying, passionate love that boggles the mind. She received his love, basked in it, and gave it right back. She was crazy about him. She respected him. She praised him frequently. And best of all, husband, she couldn't get enough of his body. His romantic behaviors made him incredibly attractive to her (Songs 5:10–16). She was all over him!

The Dialogue

Husband: I'm just not a romantic guy.

Me: Oh, OK. No problem. I guess you won't mind having zero passion and a boring, stale sex life.

Husband: She knows I love her. I don't have to be all romantic with her to prove my love.

Me: Actually, she doesn't know you love her. Without romance, she can't feel loved. So, you're wrong.

Husband: I can't afford to take her out to fancy restaurants and expensive shows.

Me: Romance can be cheap. She doesn't need the big, extravagant outings to feel romanced. Those are great, but they don't happen often enough to create ongoing romance. The little, daily actions count the most.

Husband: My dad wasn't romantic, and he and Mom had a good, solid marriage.

Me: I'll bet your mom wasn't too thrilled with his lack of romance. A good, solid marriage is a great blessing. But don't you want a great, passionate marriage with romance?

Husband: My wife is just fine with how things are in our marriage. I don't think she needs any more romance.

Me: Baloney. She's probably given up on it. Ask her—and get ready for a shock.

Husband: Doc, I'm blocking on being romantic. I have trouble when we get close, and I tend to resist emotional and physical intimacy.

Me: Let's work on the problem with you and your wife. It could be a number of factors, such as performance anxiety and lack of confidence, stress, fatigue, past unresolved pain from your family, or other relationships.

Cliff Notes on Romance

Did you remember I mentioned that there were *two* guys who would help you become more romantic? Well, I'm the second guy. I'm going to help you. Here are some surefire ideas that will get some serious romance going in your marriage.

Real kissing

Stop kissing your wife as if she's your sister. Or your aunt, Mildred. Stop delivering those unbelievably short pecks. You might as well shake her hand. Are you afraid she'll give you some kind of disease?

She is your lover and needs to be kissed as though you mean it. She needs to know she's been kissed! Start giving her open-mouth, lubricated, sucky-face kisses that last eight to ten seconds. Give her more than one kiss, too. One isn't enough to express your passionate love for your goddess, is it?

She's like Lauren Bacall in that classic Humphrey Bogart movie *To Have and Have Not*. When Bogie kisses her, Lauren purrs, "I like that. I'd like more."

Every time you kiss her, you should also do two other romantic behaviors. First, hug her. Get your arms around her in a tender embrace. Brush back her hair, and put your hands on her beautiful face. Second, after the hug and several kisses, tell her, "I love you, _________." Use her real name, not "Snookums" or "Sweet Cakes" or another one of your pet names for her.

Kiss her two or three times, hug her, and say "I love you" every chance you get—in the morning when you first awaken, when you're going off to work, when you arrive home after work, later in the evening on the couch during your talk time, and just before you go to bed.

Touching and making out

You need to be touching her in non-sexual settings throughout the week. There are all kinds of terrific touching you can do *outside* of the sexual scenario and intercourse: kissing, fondling, massaging...you know, the kind of intense touching you did back before you got married. You're married now, and God is pleased with this behavior. You can be on the couch or in bed. You may have your clothes on or off.

This kind of physical pleasuring will make her feel close to you. She'll love having you touch her without having to move on to intercourse. She'll feel cherished, and she'll appreciate that you are touching her because you love her and not just because you want intercourse.

Of course, this kind of touching also prepares you both for your times of intercourse.

Compliments

Take a tip from Solomon and compliment your wife often. You can't give her too many compliments. Compliment her physical beauty, her emotional qualities, and her spiritual sensitivity. She is very aware of her appearance and makes an effort to look nice, so tell her how great she looks. Compliment her clothes, hair, and accessories. Notice when she's wearing something you really like or something new. Occasionally take her out to ritzy places so she can dress to the nines. Cinderella needs to go to a ball sometimes.

Compliment her verbally, right to her face. Also, share compliments in e-mails, cards, and letters. She'll be thrilled to get these love notes.

Listening to her

Your lady will find it very romantic when you ask her to talk about her day, her life, her stress, her spiritual life, and how she feels about your relationship. Use the listening skills I taught in chapter 6.

Reading books together

Most men don't like to read. Be the exception. I'll bet your wife would love to read books with you and discuss them. You may read self-help Christian books such as this one or devotional books, biographies, or contemporary novels—the possibilities are great. Give it a try.

Creative dates

Take her out on a romantic date once a week. Ask her out early in the week: "Honey, would you like to go out with me this Saturday?" At least for every other date, plan something creative. Something out of the ordinary. Out of the box. Do activities she enjoys: shopping at the mall, visiting an art or craft fair, walking on the beach, having a picnic in the park, in-line skating, going to a museum, playing golf or tennis, bowling...Ask her what activities she would find romantic. Jot down what she says, and surprise her.

A Romantic Day

Here's a sample romantic day. It's what Solomon would do if he were still around.

You get up in the morning. You lean over to your wife and kiss her (more than once), tenderly embracing her. You say into her lovely ear, "I love you, _________. You're beautiful." You make the bed, get her coffee, and help get the kids going. When you leave, you hug her and kiss her several times and tell her, "I love you, _________."

You call her or e-mail her or text her during the day to tell her you love her and you're thinking about her. Mention that she looked great today. You ask her if she has any needs and what you can do.

You arrive home and do the multiple kisses, the heartfelt hug, and the "I love you, _________. I missed you." Right away, ask her what you can do for her tonight. Take care of your chores, do any jobs she's given you, help with the kids, and pitch in to clean up after dinner.

Make sure the kids are in their rooms, and ask her to sit with you for your scheduled thirty-minute talk time. Listen to her talk, share what's on your pad, and have a brief prayer together.

Enjoy a make-out session, or—maybe—if it's on the schedule, sex. And always remember: kissing, loving words, and foreplay are as much a part of—and are as important as—intercourse. Because of your romantic attention during the day, you'll find her a more responsive physical partner.

At the end of the day, give her a few more real kisses, an embrace, and a final, "I love you, _________."

Not every day will go this well, romantically speaking. Just do your best. She'll notice you are trying, and your effort will pay off in her loving response.

Build Your Happily-Ever-After Marriage

1. Husband, recall your dating days and what you did back then to be romantic. Be honest—have you lost your romantic edge? What are some examples of things you deliberately did to romance your wife, and that she loved, that you are *not* doing now?
2. Ask your wife how important romance is to her. Ask her how she thinks her feelings will change when you crank up the romance.
3. Take some time this week—maybe even right now—to read the Song of Songs together. Discuss your reactions and insights.
4. What excuses in the Dialogue section have you used to avoid being romantic?
5. Is there pain in your past or some other reason why you block on being romantic and intimate with your wife? Ask your wife which of the ideas for romance she'd like you to do on a regular basis. Ask her for other ideas she has for romance.

Chapter Eleven

MISTAKE #9: YOU CAN'T RESOLVE YOUR CONFLICTS

Learn a New Approach to Conflict

BILL AND BARBARA are an average American couple. They're decent, upstanding, and friendly people. They pay their bills, attend church, brake for squirrels, and are courteous to strangers.

Barbara is an outgoing, vivacious, and expressive person. She's a real sweetheart and fun to be with. Bill is an easygoing, hardworking guy with a dry sense of humor. He's quiet, steady, and responsible.

When life is good, they get along quite well and are happy together. But when Bill and Barbara are angry with each other, everything changes. These nice, normal individuals turn into the couple from conflict hell.

Just like some bizarre science-fiction experiment gone wrong, a shocking transformation takes place in their personalities.

Barbara, the vivacious sweetheart, becomes Barbara the screamer. She's a Doberman Pinscher with makeup. Her eyes bulge, her neck veins swell, and her voice becomes loud and shrill. Little flecks of foam spray from her mouth. She buries Bill in an avalanche of angry, intense words. She's just plain mean.

Steady, easygoing Bill becomes an escape artist. His only goal is to get away from Barbara. He's desperate to escape her clutches. He turns on the television to screen her out, but that doesn't work—no one makes televisions that loud. He goes from room to room, but she follows him like a hunter stalking prey. Finally the escape artist grabs his keys, jumps in his car, and drives away. Barbara can just make out what he's saying as he roars out of their driveway: "Finally, some peace and quiet."

When Bill returns, an uneasy silence lingers for several hours. They never bring up the conflict again or resolve it. By the next day, they are back to their normal selves.

Bill and Barbara deal with every significant conflict this same exact way: Barbara screams, and Bill escapes.

Sound familiar?

Every Couple Has a Conflict Pattern

You know something? Bill and Barbara are not the exception. They are the rule. In the first two to four years of marriage, all couples develop a deeply entrenched conflict pattern. "The screamer and the escape artist" is just one pattern. All couples have one particular way to handle conflict, and it is *not* a good, healthy way.

Your conflict pattern doesn't work! It prevents you from resolving the conflict. You never get close to facing the real issue. You don't even talk about it. The conversation is over well before you address what actually caused the conflict.

The pattern becomes the issue.

After the first thirty seconds, Barbara, the screamer, isn't thinking about the actual conflict issue or its source. She's thinking, "You weasel! You wimp! You thoughtless brute! You hurt me, and now I'm going to hurt you. I'm gonna draw blood before you can get away from me. You can run, but you can't hide, Billy Boy."

Bill, the escape artist, also isn't thinking about what started the fight. He's thinking, "I've got to get away from this Mack truck wearing a dress. If I don't, I'll be crushed to death."

What's the fight about? Nobody knows. They've forgotten.

The pattern is damaging.

This way of dealing with conflict takes another chunk out of your relationship. You are a little further apart physically, emotionally, and spiritually. The resentments and bad feelings remain and carry over to the next conflict, robbing you of couple happiness for hours or days. You seem to get over an unresolved conflict, but actually you don't. It stays right smack between you and energizes the next conflict—that is, it makes the next conflict even worse because of residual bad, hurt feelings.

Let's say you had two unresolved conflicts this past month. If you have a conflict tonight that conflict will not be just about tonight's issue. It will also be about the last two unresolved conflicts. You'll be fighting over not just one conflict, but all three!

If you want real intimacy in the new relationship you're building with your spouse, you must do two things in the area of conflict. First, dismantle your old conflict pattern. It must go because it is killing your love. Second, learn to resolve conflict in a direct and healthy way. In this chapter I'll help you do the dismantling, and I'll teach you a new way to resolve conflict.

The Patterns Go On and On

What is your conflict pattern? Besides the screamer and the escape artist, there's more. Check out these other common patterns, and see if any fit.

"We never fight."

Many couples say to me, "We haven't had an argument in our entire marriage." They say this with a straight face, and they expect me to applaud them.

They are disappointed.

I respond, "Oh, I'm sorry to hear that. Did one of you die, and you just haven't noticed?" I tell them that their conflict pattern is called "massive dual denial." It operates when both parties decide, "Let's pretend we have no conflict."

The price of no conflict? No life in the relationship. Many stuffed, buried resentments. Separate lives. In this pattern one partner gets his or her way most of the time. That's not a fun way to live for the pilot-fish partner who chooses to tag along with the big fish.

You never argue? No congratulations. You also have never had any real closeness or passion.

The tortoise and the interrogator

This is the man who refuses to talk and the woman who tries to get him to open up and deal with the issue. When conflict happens, the tortoise pulls into his protective shell and won't come out. He's angry, all right, but he won't admit it or express it. The tortoise avoids conflict like the plague. He doesn't leave; he just won't talk. He hunkers down and rides out the storm. He'd rather take a beating than deal with the conflict.

Many husbands play the part of the tortoise. They hate conflict with their wives. They know she's better at conflict. She thinks faster on her feet. Conflict makes these husbands feel out of control, and they despise that feeling. So they maintain some control by saying nothing.

The interrogator is desperate to find out what's going on in the man's head. His tortoise routine drives her crazy. She begins her interrogation, trying to get the tortoise to stick his head out of his shell. She wants him to express his feelings, to share something personal, and to face the issue. She'd settle for him saying anything at all!

The interrogator tries all kinds of approaches:

- *She asks questions.* "Are you angry? What are you angry about? Did something happen at work? Was it the tone of my voice? Was it when I dropped the ketchup bottle on your foot? What's your position on the finances? Do you want me to stay home with the kids?" She's guessing, trying to hit on what's happening in his mind. It's twenty questions. Or maybe even two hundred questions. Of course, her questions go unanswered.
- *She's sweet.* "Come on, honey, say something. You know I love you. You're special to me. Let's talk. I won't bite. Please? Please?" She even tries some affection to draw him out. But even the chance for kissy-kissy, huggy-huggy doesn't make the tortoise budge.
- *She gets ugly.* "Come out of there, sucker! I'm your wife—talk to me! How can we solve the problem if you sit there like a bump on a log? Speak! *Speak!* Have I married a mute?"

Nothing works. That's how the game is played. She tries. He resists. And they both get hurt. The conflict is never resolved. She's desperate to talk about it, but he is just as desperate *not* to talk about it.

The attorney and the emotional witness

This is the logical man and the emotional woman going toe-to-toe in a conflict. Just like a well-trained attorney, the man patiently and logically presents his case. He goes point by logical point. He expresses no emotion, only the facts as he sees them: "Now, honey, here's the way it happened. You completely misinterpreted my intentions, and then you lost your temper." He mercilessly breaks her down on the witness stand. He won't listen, he won't compromise, and he won't even seriously entertain her viewpoint. If she can't produce a logical and airtight case, he dismisses her. He's cool. He's calm. He has all the answers. He is always right. He is the source of all truth.

He is a big pain in the rear!

The woman, who is already emotional and upset because of the conflict, becomes more upset because of the attorney's approach. He won't hear her out, and he won't reflect back what she's saying. He won't attempt to offer her any understanding or see it her way. He won't consider her feelings. She becomes extremely frustrated, angry, and hurt.

The more emotional she gets, the more logical he gets. She screams, cries, and tries to get him to listen. She fails. Her rising emotional intensity further convinces him that he's right and she's wrong.

When it's all over, she's angry and hurt and feels rejected. The attorney is alone. He won the case but lost the woman. He wonders why she's so cold and quiet the next few days.

Conflict patterns abound. To identify your conflict pattern, think about how the two of you handle anger. Unless you correctly recognize and own your actions in the pattern, you'll follow the same pattern every time you have a significant conflict. That's right—every time.

Build Your Happily-Ever-After Marriage

1. What is your conflict pattern as a couple? Does one of the examples in this chapter fit you, or is your pattern different? Discuss the roles each of you plays in a conflict.
2. Where did you learn your way of behaving in conflicts? From Mom? From Dad? How did your parents deal with conflict between them? If you've been married before, talk about how you and your ex handled conflict.
3. What happens after a conflict between the two of you? If you don't resolve it, what is the impact on your relationship?
4. Agree to begin catching yourselves in your old conflict pattern. Come up with labels for your two roles.

My Conflict-Busting Formula

A man and a woman have trouble getting along when things are smooth. Living together in harmony and intimacy is tough enough when life is good and no one's upset. Why? You know why at this point in the book: because of their massive, almost unbelievable differences!

What do you think the chances are that you and your spouse will agree on what happened in a conflict and move through the resolution steps smoothly? Zero. Absolutely zero. In fact, it's even less than zero. We're talking negative numbers.

For this reason, the two of you must learn a new conflict pattern that will help you navigate through your differences to a successful conclusion.

Step #1: Catch yourselves in the act.

The first step to resolving conflict in a healthy way is to catch yourselves in your old conflict pattern—and then stop it. When you have a conflict, you will automatically move into your conflict pattern. It's entrenched. You've done it hundreds of times. It's like breathing. You're gonna do it!

The key is to work together to catch yourselves starting the pattern as soon as possible and then to stop it in its tracks. If you keep using the old conflict pattern, you'll never resolve a conflict.

The first umpteen times, you'll run right through the old pattern just as always. And, as always, you won't resolve the conflict. Later, one or both of you will realize what you've done. Bring it up: "We did it again." Talk about what you did wrong, and then restart the conflict discussion with the new approach.

As you get the hang of it, you'll begin catching the old conflict pattern earlier and earlier. You'll be able to catch yourselves as you're doing it. This will save time and limit the damage.

Try agreeing on labels in advance: "Ben, you're being the tortoise." "Betty, we're acting as if we don't have a conflict, but we do." "Escape artist, it looks like you're heading for the door." "Sara, you're being the screamer, and I'm shutting down." "Stuart, you're being the attorney, and your logic is making me emotionally intense."

Step #2: Believe your spouse.

Your new conflict pattern will be based on one essential skill: You absolutely must listen to and believe your spouse's truth.

Husbands, when your wife is talking and expressing her version of what happened and her feelings, your job is to accept what she's saying as the truth. It is *her* truth. It is the way it happened for her. Period. Two qualities of love in the classic 1 Corinthians 13 passage apply here. According to verse 5, love "seeks not its own." It's not just about you; it's also about your wife and what she thinks and feels. And verse 7 reminds us that love "believes all things." You need to give your partner the benefit of the doubt and believe what she says.

Is this easy to do? No way! Does this skill come naturally? Hardly. By nature, we do just the opposite.

Here's what usually happens. A married couple is discussing an incident that took place between them one hour before. We'll call them Bruce and Bertha. Both spouses were present during this incident. Neither spouse has a history of serious emotional illness. Neither spouse is known to be a pathological liar.

> **Bertha:** Bruce, I want to talk about what happened in the bathroom a little while ago. I'm angry that you accused me of being a gossip.
>
> **Bruce:** *[He cuts in.]* Bertha, what are you talking about? First of all, we were in the kitchen, not the bathroom.
>
> **Bertha:** I think I know what room we were in. I distinctly remember the sound of the shower.
>
> **Bruce:** That sound was the kitchen faucet running. And I certainly didn't say you were a gossip. I said I wish you hadn't told your mother what you and I talked about two nights ago.
>
> **Bertha:** You called me a gossip, and don't deny it.
>
> **Bruce:** I do deny it. I did not use that word.
>
> **Bertha:** Did so.
>
> **Bruce:** You are lying!
>
> **Bertha:** Lying? You're the one who's lying!

This conversation isn't going so well, is it? What do you think the odds are that this couple will get down to the real issues and resolve this conflict? Oh, about a million to one. And that may be overestimating the odds.

They are making the same mistakes most husbands and wives make in a conflict conversation: They are fighting over two versions of the same event. Ever do that? Of course you have. We all have, over and over again.

They are quibbling over details and semantics. Who cares if it was in the bathroom or the kitchen? That's a rabbit trail! They are incorrectly assuming that there is just one true version of what happened.

The fact is, every conflict includes two truths, two true versions of what happened. You have your truth—how you experienced the event. Your spouse has their truth—how they experienced the event. You are right. And they are right. You are both right! What is important is that the truth, to each of you, creates the feelings you both have, and those feelings are real and right.

Please understand that you and your spouse will never—and I mean *never*—agree on all the details of an event and what happened. The event could be important or trivial; it could be a conflict situation or not. One woman and one man will always see it differently. It's part of the mystery of being married.

One of you won't say, "Wow, honey! After hearing you talk, I realize I'm wrong. It happened the way you said it happened." No! Each of you experienced it differently. Two different persons always have two different perspectives and set of feelings.

So many couples get hung up on this level. Sandy and I did for years. I tried to convince Sandy that I knew the truth, and she tried to convince me that she knew the truth. This stopped the relationship cold. We didn't get any deeper. We didn't get our feelings out. In fact, we got even angrier. Neither of us felt understood by the other. We didn't resolve the conflict. We got gummed up, and we damaged our marriage. These conversations ended with both of us convinced the other was lying, rather than accepting one another's truth as being valid and real—rather than *believing* the other.

We finally figured out how to get through conflicts in a new and better way. A way that protects our marriage and actually creates more intimacy. Our way will work for you too. Here's how to do it.

Step #3: Take turns in conflict.

In my example Bruce needs to let Bertha talk, and he needs to believe that what she is saying is her truth. Here's the replay:

> **Bertha:** Bruce, I need to talk to you about something. Can you meet me at the kitchen table in ten minutes? Good.
>
> **Bertha:** *[Ten minutes later.]* Bruce, I want to talk to you about what happened in the bathroom a little while ago. I'm angry that you accused me of being a gossip.
>
> **Bruce:** *[He says nothing original. He doesn't say it was in the kitchen. He doesn't deny he called her—or implied that she was—a gossip. He does not try to straighten her out as to the "facts." No, he is too smart for that. He's learning. He thinks, "I'll do it Dr. Clarke's way."]* You heard me call you a gossip. I can see you're angry.

That's all Bruce says! He then allows Bertha to talk the whole situation out and express her feelings. With him listening, reflecting back what she says, and believing her truth, Bertha gets her anger and emotional intensity to go down. (For couples to resolve conflict, their anger must subside.)

This is the "one speaker and one listener" rule. To resolve a conflict, one spouse must be speaking and one spouse must be listening. If both spouses are speaking, they won't resolve the conflict and will damage their relationship.

When Bertha feels understood and most of her anger and hurt are out, Bruce gets his turn to present his truth. Bruce does not get his turn to speak until Bertha gives him the go-ahead. He doesn't start when *he* feels ready to talk. He starts when *she* feels ready to listen. That will be when she feels understood and believed. If Bruce starts too soon, Bertha won't be ready to listen.

After a short break to let Bertha's feeling of being understood settle and become solid, Bruce talks. Bertha listens, reflects back what she hears, and believes his truth. Of course, his truth will be different from hers. He might say:

> I'm sorry for what I did to make you feel angry and hurt. I didn't mean to, but it happened. Please forgive me. What I was trying to say was I'm angry that you told your mom about the financial talk we had two nights ago. I know you didn't mean anything by it, but I feel like that's our personal business.

Bruce validates Bertha's feelings and point of view. He makes sure she feels that he understands and believes her. He apologizes. Only then does he share his side of things. He does not try to refute her view and talk her out of her feelings. He is following 1 Peter 3:7 and being gentle and respectful of her.

Let's put all this together. Catching yourselves in your old conflict pattern is good, but it is not good enough. Listening to and believing your spouse's truth is also good, but it's not good enough, either. These steps are not good enough, because two more major steps are necessary for working through a conflict.

Step #4: Use the stop-and-start method.

You need to stop temporarily when you've lost it. When I say *lost it*, I mean at least one of you is breaking the rules. You're not listening. You're distracted. You're interrupting. You're too angry, and you're yelling. You're making personal attacks. You're clamming up and shutting down. You're reverting to your role in the old conflict pattern, and you are not believing your partner's truth.

When a conflict conversation gets off track, even a little bit, you need to *stop temporarily.* Unless you stop briefly, you are not going to be able to gear down and get back on track. The conflict will get worse, and you'll end up making a bigger mess. It's approaching the point of no return.

Can you imagine the following? One of you says, "I'm angry. I'm out of control. But wait! I'm noticing I have a problem. I'm regaining my poise and control, and I'm lowering my voice. Sorry about that, my dear. Now, where were we?" Dream on. It doesn't work this way. No one can do that. When you lose it, you get mean and nasty. So do I.

Every significant conflict, like any good conversation, is a process. You do not get through it in one unbroken sitting. You need to take breaks when you get off track. Get alone to cool off and process. Let understanding resonate and take hold.

The issues and feelings that arise in a conflict are deep and make you vulnerable. Both the husband and wife need breaks to think, evaluate, search their souls, talk to God, consider each other's point of view, pull themselves together, and get a grip.

A healthy conflict conversation could last several hours. It's more likely to last a couple of days, especially if it's a big conflict. Ideally you want to clear your anger out by the end of the first day (Eph. 4:26), but the rest of the process usually lasts longer.

You must revisit the issue until you've worked it through completely. This will be particularly tough for the spouse who wants to resolve the conflict right away. "Right away" and marital conflict don't go together. Most men are particularly slow processors in a conflict.

Take breaks! Conflict is like a grueling physical sport. It could be an Olympic event, but who'd want to watch? Talk through a conflict in short spurts.

Take a break when you mess up—when you catch yourselves in your conflict pattern, when you start fighting over whose version is the truth, when one of you starts yelling, when one of you isn't listening and reflecting.

Take a break after one partner has shared their side. Let the fragile understanding you just achieved take root.

Take a break after both of you have shared and understood your two versions of the truth. This break is good preparation for the final step in the conflict-resolution process.

Step #5: Let's make a deal.

Many times, talking through your feelings and points of view is enough to resolve a conflict. You don't have to do anything else. But sometimes you both need to agree on a deal, a plan of action to handle the situation.

Making a deal is important. So take a break after you've achieved understanding of your two truths. Set a time to come back together. Process on your own. Think of possible solutions and compromises.

When you return to talk, pray for God's help. Make a deal that is specific and measurable. Don't say, "Let's try harder." No one knows what that means.

In our previous example of Bruce and Bertha, the compromise might be, "Let's agree to not share any financial information with anyone without one another's permission."

Make every deal on a trial basis. If it works, great. If it doesn't, return to the table and renegotiate. Either spouse can call for a renegotiation.

If you don't learn how to resolve conflict, your marriage will slowly die. It will choke on smoldering resentments and bitterness. If you do learn how to resolve conflict, your marriage will be free to grow and thrive. It will be alive and refreshed with closeness and passion and joy and fun.

Build Your Happily-Ever-After Marriage

1. Discuss a recent conflict in which you had two totally different versions of what happened. How did that conflict turn out?
2. Do you believe me when I say every conflict has two truths? If you doubt this, why? What kind of damage have you done to your marriage by fighting over two versions of the truth?
3. What might keep you from following the five conflict strategies in this chapter? For each of the strategies listed, ask yourself, "What might keep me/us from: avoiding my old conflict patterns; believing my spouse; taking turns in conflict; using the stop-and-start method; and making a deal?"
4. Which of the five strategies will cause you the most trouble? Commit together to practicing this strategy when you have your next conflict the minute it begins or may begin. Pray right now that God will help you improve your conflict-resolution skills.

Chapter Twelve

MISTAKE #10: YOU'RE NOT SPIRITUALLY BONDING

Put God at the Center of Your Relationship

MEETING NEEDS. LEARNING how to communicate. Making time for each other. Making your spouse your priority immediately after your relationship with God. Being assertive and not allowing mistreatment. Becoming sensitive and gentle. Working to be sexually responsive. Being romantic as a way of life. Resolving conflicts.

All these behaviors are important in the process of building your new marriage. But you must develop one more behavior, one more area of intimacy, to have a passionate and truly Christian marriage. It is spiritual intimacy.

When you are spiritually intimate, the power and presence of God operates at full strength in your marriage.

The two of you are no longer loving in human strength alone. God Himself is doing the loving. He will work through each of you to produce the best and deepest love possible on earth.

"One Flesh" Intimacy

In Genesis 2:24, God provides His definition of heterosexual marital intimacy: "Therefore a man will leave his father and his mother and be joined to his wife, and they will become one flesh." *One flesh* describes the complete union of a husband and a wife in three areas:

1. Physical: two bodies
2. Intellectual/emotional: two minds and two sets of feelings
3. Spiritual: two personal relationships with the Lord

This third area, spiritual intimacy, is the driving force behind the one-flesh relationship. Spiritual intimacy taps the power of God and puts it to work in your marriage. If you want to love each other with God's love, you must be connected to Him as a couple. You must join spiritually.

Joining spiritually is the secret to genuine, lasting intimacy in marriage. I call this *spiritual bonding.* Spiritual bonding is consistently placing God at the very center of your marriage and growing ever closer to Him as a couple.

Here's how to get started on your adventure of spiritual bonding.

You Both Must Be Christians

To bond spiritually, both spouses must be spiritually alive. That means that both spouses must be Christians. A Christian is someone who has a personal relationship with the one, true God, the God of the Bible, through believing in His Son, Jesus Christ.

The only way to God is through Jesus (John 14:6). God sent Jesus to die for your sins, to sacrifice His life so you could have a relationship with God: "For God so loved the world that He gave His only begotten Son, that whoever believes in Him should not perish, but have eternal life" (John 3:16). As 1 Corinthians 15:3–4 states, to become a Christian and know God in a personal way, you have to believe three facts about Jesus Christ: "that Christ died for our sins according to the Scriptures, and that He was buried, and that He was raised on the third day."

If you have never made the decision to believe that Jesus died and rose from the dead, you can do it right now by saying the words in this brief prayer (but know it is not the words that will save you but your heart attitude and trust in Christ):

> *Dear God,*
>
> *I know I am a sinner. I've made many mistakes in my life. I realize my sin separates me from You, the holy God. I believe Your Son, Jesus, died for my sins, was buried, and rose from the dead. I give my life to You now.*

If your spouse isn't ready to become a Christian yet, I still recommend strongly that the two of you begin a spiritual bonding process. Along the way, your spouse can come to know God through Jesus.

The Husband Needs to Lead

God's design (see Ephesians 5:22–24) is for the husband to lead his wife in every area of the relationship, including the spiritual. Of course, the wife is fully involved in the spiritual bonding behaviors. You do them together. But, husband, you are responsible for making sure three spiritual bonding actions happen on a regular basis: prayer, spiritual conversations, and Bible reading and study.

Ask a solid, Christian, happily married man to hold you accountable in this area of spiritual leadership. If you can find a man who is providing spiritual leadership to his wife in a marriage that is working well and is mutually satisfying, sign him up as your mentor and accountability partner immediately. This could be your pastor, an older man in the church, or a friend around your age.

Your wife will be thrilled with your spiritual leadership. Your marriage will improve dramatically. You'll be modeling for your kids how to build a Christian marriage. Best of all, God will be pleased, and He will bless you.

How to Pray

You can pray as a couple in many different, creative ways. The following practical guidelines can get you started.

Schedule three five-minute prayer times a week.

You can pray for the first five minutes of your scheduled thirty-minute talk times. This not only makes prayer more convenient but also creates a deeper mood and warms you up for your conversations.

Choose one special place in your home to pray.

Using the place where you have your talk times makes the most sense. After prayer, just stay where you are and move into conversation. This place must be private and quiet. Get the kids out of your hair. This is not family devotions; it's couple prayer time.

When you pray, hold hands.

This connects you and is an outward expression of your one-flesh relationship.

Pray aloud.

You're not spiritually bonding if you pray silently. Listening to your partner talk to God is an important part of sharing his or her bond with God.

At least one spouse commonly struggles with praying aloud. That spouse can pray silently for one or two weeks. The partner praying silently may squeeze the other's hand when finished.

In the beginning neither of you will be praying on a deep or personal level. You'll bring up topics that are important but not that deep and intimate. Gradually increase your transparency when you pray.

Husband, you may be too uncomfortable or intimidated to pray in front of your wife. She talks better than you, and she probably prays better than you. She may be closer to God than you. The truth is, she won't ever criticize your prayers. After your first aloud prayer with her, she won't say, "Is that the best you can do, Bob? Why, that's the prayer of a sixth-grader! I had no idea how spiritually shallow you are!" Of course she won't. She will be happy and impressed beyond words that you are praying with her.

Make a list, and take turns in prayer.

Husband, have a pad with you and jot down the requests you each want to bring before God. When you have a list, divide it up between you and pray one at a time. Here's a sample list one couple used during a prayer time:

- The church's building fund
- Guidance for the pastors at church
- The next-door neighbor's illness
- Patience with a supervisor at work
- Money to pay the taxes
- The children:
  Dan—his grades, especially in math
  Cindy—wisdom and protection in her dating relationships
  Beth—more friends at youth group and at school
- The marriage:
  to spend more quality time together

to keep praying three times a week
to have sex at least once a week [his request]

- That Mike would become a Christian

Your prayer list will serve also as a written record of God's faithfulness. As God answers your prayers (not always with a yes), jot down the answers and the date of the answers.

Praise God together.

Spend a few minutes at each prayer session praising God for who He is and what He's done for you and your family. As we read again and again in the Psalms—indeed, throughout the entire Bible—God is worthy of praise and loves to be worshipped in this way.

As you continue to pray together, you'll find that you'll both be more open and personal in what you say to God. You'll pray for your real concerns and the deep desires of your hearts. You'll share intimate things that you will never share in front of any other person.

How to Talk Spiritually

You can spend part of your scheduled talk times talking about spiritual things. Most married couples don't do this—and they miss out on some wonderful spiritual bonding. The spiritual is the most important part of your life, so sharing it will create some pretty intense intimacy. Probably even some passion. Would you like some intimacy and passion? Talk spiritually on a regular basis.

Here's a brief list of spiritual topics you can talk about as a couple:

- What God revealed to you through the pastor's sermon
- How God wants you to apply the sermon
- How God wants you to serve in your church
- How your service in the church is going
- What you're learning in your personal devotions
- How God guided you today
- How God blessed you today
- A verse you read this morning
- How you're doing spiritually right now
- How you're struggling with God and why
- How God wants you to share Christ with your neighbor
- How Satan was all over you today and what happened
- How God is testing you at your job
- How each of you is doing spiritually

I'm talking about discipleship. As you follow Jesus, you are discipling each other!

You can help each other grow spiritually. Your marriage ought to be the most important discipling relationship in your life. It can be, if you begin to talk about spiritual things.

How to Read and Study the Bible

The Bible is God's Word. Think of that—God's actual Word! It is incredibly powerful, and you can apply that power to your marriage by reading and studying and applying it. Also, as a bonus, the Bible can cut through all the barriers between the two of you and bring you closer to each other than you've ever been:

> For the word of God is alive, and active, and sharper than any two-edged sword, piercing even to the division of soul and spirit, of joints and marrow, and able to judge the thoughts and intents of the heart.
>
> —Hebrews 4:12

If this isn't a great description of intimacy, I don't know what is! If you read and study God's Word together, it will reveal who you really are. When two hearts are revealed, you have intimacy—an intimacy all the better and deeper because God gave it to you through His Word.

You can probably think of many helpful ways to read and study the Bible together. I recommend you start by following this simple and effective plan: read on Monday, discuss on Friday.

Read on Monday

Sit down early in the week—we'll say Monday—and read aloud the passage of Scripture you have selected. Choose a brief passage, no more than three verses. Many new versions and study Bibles break the verses and chapters into sections by topics. Take a moment or two to silently meditate on the passage. Either aloud or silently, ask God to speak to you through His Word. He'll answer that prayer. He promised that the Holy Spirit would reveal truth in His Word (John 14:26; 16:13–14).

Then take turns briefly discussing your response to the passage. What does it mean? What is God saying to you? What thoughts or emotions does the passage trigger in you?

The woman commonly has an immediate reaction, and the man may not have much to say. I know that comes as a shock to you, wife. He'll say, "I don't know," or, "I'm not sure." That's fine. Don't worry about it. A man takes longer to process information. Don't press him for a response right away. Don't say, "What's your reaction to this passage, Bob? It's the Word of God, Bob! God and I are waiting, Bob!" Back off and give him time to find a reaction. He has until Friday.

At the end of this meeting, do three things:

1. Schedule a time to discuss the passage on Friday.
2. Each of you pray aloud that God will speak to you through what you read over the next four or five days.

3. Each of you write the passage on a three-by-five card or in your electronic device. Agree to read the passage at least once a day and meditate on it over the next four or five days. You could make this brief meditation part of your personal daily quiet time with the Lord. You are preparing for Friday. As you meditate and pray for insight from God, make a note of what God impresses on you about the verses. By Friday you'll each have a few notes written down.

Discuss on Friday

On Friday meet again to share the results of your meditation and reflection. At this second meeting, you'll both have some things to say. The woman will have more to say because she always has more to say. The man will have something to say because he's had time to process.

You each read what you've written in your notes about the passage. You may share what the passage means for your individual life, marriage, family, career, or service in the church. Maybe God is comforting and encouraging you through the passage. Maybe God is confronting you through the passage. Maybe God wants you to apply the truth in the passage in a certain way in the coming week.

Can you see how this plan has the power to create some stimulating spiritual conversations? God will speak to you through the passages you select. By sharing this intimate, spiritual information with your spouse, you will be drawn closer together.

You aren't meant to do this "read and discuss" plan every week. No couple is that spiritually minded. Besides, who has the time for that? I recommend doing it once every two months. Go ahead, try it. You'll like it. I know God will like it, and He will bless you for reading and discussing His precious Word.

In God's plan for marriage, sexual intercourse is to be the beautiful and regularly occurring one-flesh result (the climax, literally) of a married couple's ongoing emotional and spiritual intimacy. Every few days (or whatever time frame you choose as a team), the emotional and spiritual needs you have met prepare you to be one in intercourse.

Build Your Happily-Ever-After Marriage

1. What do you know about the practice of spiritual bonding? Have you read anything about this or heard about it in church or in the Christian media?
2. What kind of spiritual bonding behaviors do you presently practice as a couple?
3. Do you both know God through His Son, Jesus, in the way I described? If not, are you ready to begin a relationship with God now, or will you begin an earnest, honest search? If you have honest problems and questions about beginning a relationship with God, will you find a reliable, knowledgeable person to help you?
4. Husband, are you willing to take the lead in this area of spiritual bonding? What will make this hard for you?
5. Wife, how do you feel about letting your husband take the lead spiritually in your marriage? What will be difficult for you in this?
6. Which of the three bonding behaviors (prayer, talking about spiritual things, and reading and studying the Bible) are you willing to start doing this week?

Part III

It's Time to Live Happily Ever After

Chapter Thirteen

GOOD-BYE, RITUALS HELLO, INTIMACY

I HATE TO TELL you this, but there's just about a 100 percent guarantee that you're going to die before your time. Me too. We have very little chance of living to a ripe old age. Why? Because of all the normal, everyday things that are killing us! Every couple of weeks, another newspaper article or television news report warns us of the fatal effects of some new and hideous health hazard.

High cholesterol kills. Too much salt kills. Too much sugar kills. Too much fat in our diet kills. Not enough fat in our diet kills. Red meat kills. Mercury in fish kills. Killer bees from South America are coming to kill us all. (They've been coming for twenty years. They're slow bees, but they'll eventually make it.)

My own mother played a role in killing me. She fed me margarine throughout my childhood. Turns out it's a killer! It turns into plastic in our arteries.

Pollution of the air and water kills. Disease-carrying mosquitoes kill. Secondhand smoke kills. Nonstick coating on cookware kills. Even vegetables aren't safe, because they're sprayed with deadly pesticides.

I was dealing pretty well with all these killers until just recently. Then I saw a television story that said the wrappers for fast food are also killers. That was it. That sent me over the edge.

The truth is, I really don't worry about all these killers. I take all the dire reports about them with a grain of salt. (But just a grain; too much will kill me.) If they are killing us, they are taking an awfully long time doing it. Yeah, they might just get us in our seventies or eighties. Besides, no one can avoid all these things. We have to eat something, or we'll starve to death before one of them kills us.

But I do worry about one killer. It's the number-one killer of all marriages. Since I make my living working with married couples, I've been fighting this killer for years. It's boredom. I'm on a crusade to stamp out boredom in marriages.

As I explained in chapters 1 and 2, the standard marital contract leads to rigid, patterned rituals. The rituals—doing things the same old female and male way—lead to a terrible boredom. After you've paralyzed your marriage with boredom, you turn to intimacy substitutes—persons or activities that take the place of the lost passion with your marriage partner.

We've been exploring a strategy that will beat boredom and create an exciting, spontaneous, and fresh love between you and your spouse. You've already read most of the strategy. We've taken a good bite out of boredom by correcting the classic wife and husband mistakes. You're well on your way to a new and better marriage.

Now we need to finish the job. I'm going to help you shake up your remaining rituals and peel away your intimacy substitutes.

Shoot Your Old Marriage

Tired of being bored? Throw out your old marriage and build a new one that works. The two of you can do it together! I tell couples all the time, "Your relationship is awful. It bores me to death just listening to you describe it. Please, put it out of its misery. Take it out back, shoot it, and bury it. Let's start over."

Rebuilding with your marriage partner is God's answer. It won't be easy, but it's what God wants, and He'll help you do it. Part of growing as a Christian is putting off the "old self" and putting on the "new self" (Col. 3:9–10). The same thing is needed in your marriage. You have to put off the old marriage and put on the new one.

You may be on the verge of giving up. Don't! You may think you're stuck with the marriage you have. You're not—unless you want to be.

God wants your marriage to work. He wants you to turn over every stone in an effort to build a new marriage. If you demonstrate real faith in God and take the necessary rebuilding steps, He will bless your efforts.

Attack Your Rituals

Study your relationship and discover all the rituals. Reread chapters 1 and 2 to get some good clues; then study your relationship to discover and label all the rituals. Finding them will not be that tough once you start looking. You're like two trees in a petrified forest. Nothing ever changes. The time has come to change your old, boring, intimacy-sapping routines.

Change your morning routine.

Get up earlier and share coffee or orange juice together. If you have kids, get up before they do. Beat them to the punch! Or keep them in their rooms while you share a few quiet minutes together.

Shower together occasionally. Two persons can fit in most showers. Why, that's perfect, because there's two of you! I've gone door-to-door in communities all across the United States to research the size of showers. I've found that almost all showers can hold two individuals. But very few married couples ever get in there together. Come on!

Showering together in the morning will start your day with a jolt. It's a jolt you need. You can do a lot of things in a shower besides taking a shower, if you know what I mean.

When you leave home, lay a long, wet one on your spouse. A real gum-scorcher of a kiss. A teeth rattler. You're kissing your baby! You're kissing your stud man! And what comes along with that big old whopper of a kiss? Two or three more show-stopping kisses, a sensual embrace, and an "I love you, _________."

I know married couples who don't kiss in the morning as they prepare to go their separate ways. Standing only ten or fifteen feet apart, they say to each other, "Hugs and kisses." That's about exciting as being in the bedroom and instead of touching each other, merely saying, "Foreplay and sex."

Change your evening routine.

Go home, carry your television set to the front door, kick the door open, and throw that stupid set into the front yard. Get rid of it! If you won't do that, cancel your cable or satellite service. You don't need 150 channels.

At the very least, don't turn on the television until *after* you have communicated and connected as a couple. Don't give your best hours to that idiot box. You know what it makes you? An idiot!

When you get back together in the evening, show you're glad to see each other. Do the multiple kisses, the tender hug, and the "I love you, _________." Cook dinner together. Clean up after dinner together. Take a walk around the neighborhood. Play a card or board game, just the two of you.

Early in the evening get rid of the kids and carve out thirty minutes to be together. No distractions, just *the two of you.* Don't let the kids interrupt you. Ignore their usual pathetic excuses to avoid going to bed. In response to the classic "I need a drink of water," say, "I need you to stay in bed. If you die of thirst, I'm sorry."

Nothing is more stimulating and unpredictably intimate than conversational and spiritual time together as a couple. Read a couples' devotional, talk about what happened during the day, share what God is doing in your lives, pray, read the Bible, and do some massaging and making out.

Change your bedroom and weekend routine.

Change the side of the bed where you usually sleep. That'll shake things up! Experiment and try new things in your sexual relationship. Be creative and have some fun. Husband, rig up a branch in the bedroom and start swinging like our old friend, the gibbon. If you can't find a branch that will work, use the ceiling fan. If these ideas are too far out, come up with better ideas.

Go out on a romantic date once a week and do activities you've never done before or haven't done in a long time. Take turns surprising each other. Rent a sailboat. Fly a kite. Play miniature golf. Take in a community theater play. Volunteer at a homeless shelter.

PEEL AWAY YOUR INTIMACY SUBSTITUTES

Just about every married person will find himself or herself an intimacy substitute—an activity intended to replace intimacy with the spouse; it may even be a person. In the first seven to ten years of a marriage (sometimes sooner), you realize you can't meet each other's needs. You don't know how!

Your rituals have drained most of the passion out of your relationship. Boredom has set in with a vengeance. Since you still have a deep need for passion and intimacy, you both turn from the relationship and develop substitutes.

These substitutes help you avoid your partner (and the pain and frustration of unmet needs) and meet some superficial needs. But they cause more and more separation and loneliness in the marriage.

Television addicts

You are mesmerized and utterly fascinated by your television set. You flip it on as soon as you can and leave it on as long as you can. Often, you're not even watching it. It's just background noise. The people on television are your friends and companions. You are living through them. And they're not even real!

Television is your escape, your relaxation, and your entertainment. It's turning your mind into mush. You are a zombie! Is television really that fulfilling? No. Is it better than nothing? Yeah. Yeah, it is.

Computer hacks and phone junkies

Tippy, tippy, tippy on the keyboard all night long. You send e-mails and texts. You read and send e-mails. You tweet and post on Facebook. You play games. You spend time in chat rooms talking to persons you don't even know. You surf the Internet checking on your investments and shopping for great deals. Your mission is to seek out new worlds and new civilizations. To boldly go where no person has gone before. To reach level three of the new game you just installed.

You are powerful. You have unlimited knowledge at your command. With the stroke of a key, you can know the mating ritual of the bobtailed booby. Actually, *you* are the booby! You are wasting hours of time on the computer and on your phone. You are unavailable to your spouse. You are a techno dud! You are in love with your technology. Admit it!

Pet lovers

You give your pet more time, talk, and affection than you give your spouse. When you get home, you walk right past your partner, and you're all over your pet: "Hello, baby. Did you miss me? I love my sweetie." You stroke, you massage, and you whisper sweet nothings. You walk your pet, you feed your pet, and you play with your pet. You even kiss (yuck!) your pet, don't you, Dog Breath?

If your spouse has a bad cold, you say, "Too bad. I hope you feel better." If your pet gets the sniffles, you're at the vet in record time: "Doctor, help me. Snuggles is sick!"

Loving and demonstrating love to a pet is a whole lot easier than loving and expressing love to a human, isn't it?

Putterers

You just can't sit still and relax in your own home. You have ants in your pants. You're always moving, always doing, and always puttering. You feel good when you are being productive and completing jobs. You can't stand to leave any job undone. All the unfinished jobs call to you. Men putter on the lawn, in the garage, and with their cars. Women putter by cleaning, performing a million household jobs, and doing crafts, or creating photo albums.

You putter away the whole evening. Your spouse asks you to join him or her, but you don't. You have to putter!

These are just a few examples of intimacy substitutes. The list could continue: kidaholics, workaholics, bookaholics, golfaholics, fishingaholics, huntingaholics, churchaholics, etc. Often an intimacy substitute can be a destructive addiction: pornography (now so easy to view on the Internet), another man or woman, alcohol, drugs, gambling, food, cigarettes, etc.

These substitutes, like all substitutes serving in the place of the real thing, are cheap and unsatisfying. Why would you settle for a pathetic imitation when you can have real, honest-to-goodness intimacy? I'll tell you why. You hang on to your substitute because you don't think your partner will ever meet your real needs. You've given up on that dream!

In your old relationship you're right. It'll never happen. In your new relationship, the one God will help you build, it can happen. It will happen—if you both work at it.

Make It to Ever After

God says in Genesis 2:24 and Ephesians 5:22–33 that the marriage relationship is to meet your deepest human needs. That's why He created marriage. That's what it's for! If you don't have intimacy, which meets vital, God-given needs, something is wrong. Your marriage is not fulfilling God's design and purpose for you.

So how do you get there? First, shoot the old marriage. Second, attack the rituals. Third, peel away the substitutes.

How do you do that last part? Start by identifying and admitting you've chosen an intimacy substitute. Don't deny it. Nearly everyone has one. My substitutes are reading, sports on television, and my career. Then put your substitute in its place. If it is not bad in itself, its place is beneath your partner on the priority list. Make sure you connect with your spouse *first*; when you meet your spouse's needs to their satisfaction and happiness, then you can enjoy your substitute. I'm not suggesting you get rid of your substitute unless it is a sin. Just relax with your substitute after you have met each other's needs.

Talk and touch and meet needs as a couple first. That's what the regularly scheduled thirty-minute talk times are designed for. Then you can do whatever you want to do the rest of the evening. Most spouses do their substitutes first and then, at the end of the evening, give each other the leftovers. Meeting each other's needs and connecting intimately is impossible when you're exhausted. If you do this, you've given your best hours to your substitute!

Agree that your old relationship is over. Let it go. Say a prayer of farewell over it and scatter the ashes. With God's help, start building a new relationship by changing your routines and dropping your intimacy substitutes.

When you started reading this book, I'll bet you wondered if you could ever live happily ever after with your spouse. At this point you know this kind of wonderful, intimate relationship is within your reach. It does take work, but you can achieve it!

Fix the ten mistakes and face each other in true intimacy, just as you've learned how to do now, and step into the happily-ever-after marriage you were always intended to have.

Build Your Happily-Ever-After Marriage

1. How is your marriage? Be honest. On a scale of one to ten (one being super boring and ten being thrilling), how would it score? What has made it as boring as it is?
2. Are you willing to shoot your old marriage and start over? Pray right now, and tell God you're ready to build a new marriage.
3. Talk specifically about how you can change your morning routine, your evening routine, your bedroom routine, and your weekend routine.
4. If you have an addiction, agree now that you and your spouse will seek professional help to defeat it.
5. Tell your spouse (as if he or she doesn't know already!) what your intimacy substitute is. Are you willing to put your spouse above it and give him or her your best time, never leftovers?

RESOURCES

OTHER BOOKS BY David Clarke:

- *Married But Lonely: Seven Steps You Can Take With or Without Your Spouse's Help*, with William G. Clarke
- *I Don't Want a Divorce: A 90-Day Guide to Saving Your Marriage*, with William G. Clarke
- *What to Do When Your Spouse Says, I Don't Love You Anymore: An Action Plan to Regain Confidence, Power, and Control*
- *Kiss Me Like You Mean It: Solomon's Crazy in Love How-to Manual*
- *A Marriage After God's Own Heart: Achieving the Ultimate: Spiritual Intimacy in Your Marriage*
- *Men Are Clams, Women Are Crowbars: Understand Your Differences, and Make Them Work*

- A study guide for couples and groups/classes is also available.
- *Winning the Parenting War: A Battle Plan for Securing Victory on the Home Front*
- *I'm Not OK, and Neither Are You: The 6 Steps to Emotional Freedom*
- *The Top Ten Most Outrageous Couples of the Bible,* with William G. Clarke

To schedule a seminar, order Dr. Clarke's books, set up an in-person or telephone advice session, schedule a marriage intensive, or access his speaking schedule, please contact:

David Clarke Seminars
www.davidclarkeseminars.com
1-888-516-8844

or

Marriage and Family Enrichment Center
6505 North Himes Avenue
Tampa, FL 33614

ABOUT THE AUTHORS

DAVID E. CLARKE, PhD, is a Christian psychologist, speaker, and the author of nine books, including *Married but Lonely*. A graduate of Dallas Theological Seminary and Western Conservative Baptist Seminary in Portland, Oregon, he has been in private practice for twenty-five years. He lives in Florida with his wife, Sandy, and their four children.

William G. Clarke, MA, has been a marriage and family therapist for over thirty years. He is a graduate of the University of Southern California and the California Family Study Center, where he earned his master's degree. With his wife, he served with Campus Crusade for Christ (CRU) for nine years. He is the founder of the Marriage and Family Enrichment Center in Tampa, Florida. He lives in Tampa with his wife, Kathleen.